BANFF NATIONAL PARK
TRAVEL GUIDE
2024-2025

DIANE W. CLARK

Copyright © 2024 by Diane W. Clark

All rights reserved. No part of this book may be reproduced, distributed, or transmitted in any form or by any means, including photocopying, recording, or other electronic or mechanical methods, without the prior written permission of the publisher, except in the case of brief quotations embodied in critical reviews and specific other noncommercial uses permitted by copyright law

TABLE OF CONTENTS

INTRODUCTION

Banff National Park is one of those places that stays with you long after you leave. Nestled in the heart of the Canadian Rockies, it's a natural wonder with its towering mountains, turquoise lakes, and endless forests. It's the kind of place that pulls you in with its beauty and keeps you coming back for more.

I'd always been someone who loved to travel, always looking for the next adventure. But Banff wasn't originally on my radar until a simple conversation with a friend changed everything. We were talking about dream vacations when he mentioned a contest he'd seen online about Banff National Park. The idea of visiting such a stunning place intrigued me, so I decided to enter. I didn't expect much, but then something amazing happened—I won! The prize was a free trip to Banff, and just like that, my journey to this incredible place began.

From the moment I stepped out of the airport, Banff took my breath away. The air was crisp and fresh, and the mountains seemed to stretch endlessly into the sky. The drive through lush forests and past clear rivers was like something out of a postcard, and when I arrived at Lake Louise, I was stunned. The water was the clearest turquoise I'd ever seen, surrounded by snow-covered peaks. It was one of those moments when nature's beauty feels almost unreal.

The next few days were filled with adventure. I hiked through dense forests, kayaked on peaceful glacial lakes, and even got close to some of the local wildlife—elk and deer, who seemed almost as curious about me as I was about them. Banff felt like a place where nature and people existed together in harmony. The friendly locals only added to that feeling, sharing their deep love for the park and how important it is to keep it preserved for future generations.

One night, sitting by a campfire under a sky full of stars, I realized that Banff was more than just a trip. It was an experience that changed how I saw the world. The peace I found there and the connection I felt with nature were unforgettable. That's when I decided to write this guide, hoping to capture the magic of Banff for others.

In this book, you'll find everything you need to know to explore Banff National Park, from the best hiking trails to where to spot wildlife. I want you to experience the same awe and wonder that I did, to connect with nature and find peace in its beauty. Banff is a place that will inspire you, recharge your spirit, and leave you with memories that last a lifetime.

So, keep reading, and let me take you on a journey through one of the most stunning places on earth. Banff is waiting for you.

About Banff National Park

Banff National Park is a breathtaking place located in the heart of the Canadian Rockies in Alberta, Canada. It's Canada's oldest national park, established in 1885, and it covers over 6,600 square kilometers of rugged mountains, clear lakes, dense forests, and glaciers. The park is part of a larger UNESCO World Heritage site, recognized for its stunning natural beauty and its importance in preserving the unique landscapes of the Rocky Mountains.

The moment you arrive in Banff, it's hard not to be impressed by the sheer scale of the mountains that surround you. Peaks like Mount Rundle and Cascade Mountain dominate the skyline, towering over the town of Banff and the surrounding valleys. Whether you're driving along the winding roads or hiking on one of the many trails, the scenery is constantly changing and always awe-inspiring.

One of the most famous spots in the park is Lake Louise, known for its striking turquoise water that comes from the glaciers above. No matter how many pictures you've seen, nothing compares to standing on the shore and seeing the lake in person, framed by towering snow-capped mountains. It's a place that feels almost otherworldly, and it's one of the main reasons so many people are drawn to Banff.

Nearby, Moraine Lake offers another spectacular view. The deep blue color of the water, set against the backdrop of the Valley of the Ten Peaks, is something that stays with you long after you've left. These lakes are popular for activities like canoeing, photography, or simply sitting quietly and soaking in the beauty of nature.

Banff is also known for its wildlife. The park is home to a wide range of animals, including elk, deer, bighorn sheep, and even bears. It's common to see wildlife along the roadside or while hiking, which makes every moment in the park feel like an adventure. Just remember to keep your distance and respect the animals, as this is their home.

For those who love outdoor activities, Banff is a dream destination. In the summer, there are endless opportunities for hiking, from easy walks along lakeshores to challenging trails that take you up into the high alpine areas with panoramic views of the Rockies. There are also chances to go kayaking, fishing, and even rock climbing. In the winter, Banff transforms into a wonderland for skiing, snowboarding, snowshoeing, and ice skating on frozen lakes.

The town of Banff itself is a charming, lively place with plenty of shops, restaurants, and galleries to explore. It's a great base for your adventures in the park, offering comfortable places to stay and a welcoming atmosphere. Even in town, you're never far from nature—the surrounding mountains are always visible, reminding you of the beauty that waits just outside your door.

One of the special things about Banff is how easy it is to feel connected to the natural world. Whether you're hiking through forests filled with the scent of pine, standing on the shores of a glacial lake, or gazing up at a star-filled sky, it's a place that invites you to slow down and appreciate the simple wonders of nature.

Banff National Park is more than just a place to visit—it's a place that leaves a lasting impression. It's where you can find peace, adventure, and a deeper connection to the natural world. If you're looking for a destination that combines stunning scenery, outdoor activities, and a sense of tranquility, Banff is a place you shouldn't miss. Whether it's your first visit or your tenth, there's always something new to discover in this remarkable corner of the world.

Why you should Visit Banff National Park

Banff National Park is a place that should be on everyone's travel list. The park offers something for every type of traveler, whether you're someone who loves outdoor adventures, peaceful moments in nature, or just wants to experience one of the most beautiful places in the world.

The first reason to visit Banff is its stunning natural beauty. Everywhere you turn, you're surrounded by towering mountains, crystal-clear lakes, and dense forests. Places like Lake Louise and Moraine Lake are famous for their turquoise waters that seem almost unreal. These lakes, framed by snow-covered peaks, are some of the most photographed spots in the world, but seeing them in person is even more special. The beauty of Banff is the kind that takes your breath away, and it's something you will never forget.

Another reason to visit Banff is the chance to connect with nature in a way that feels peaceful and calming. The fresh mountain air, the sound of rushing rivers, and the sight of wildlife roaming freely all create an atmosphere that makes you feel far from the stress of everyday life. It's a place where you can slow down and just enjoy the simple things—like a walk through the woods, the reflection of the mountains on a lake, or a quiet moment watching the sun set behind the peaks.

For those who love outdoor activities, Banff is like a playground. In the summer, there are hiking trails for all levels, from easy walks around lakes to more challenging climbs up to stunning viewpoints. You can go kayaking, canoeing, or even horseback riding through the scenic trails. In the winter, Banff turns into a snowy wonderland perfect for skiing, snowboarding, or ice skating on frozen lakes. No matter what time of year you visit, there is always something to do outdoors, making it a great destination for adventure lovers.

Banff is also home to an incredible variety of wildlife. If you enjoy seeing animals in their natural habitat, Banff won't disappoint. You might spot elk grazing by the side of the road, bighorn sheep climbing rocky cliffs, or even a black bear wandering through the forest. The wildlife in Banff is one of the park's highlights, and every encounter feels like a special moment.

The town of Banff itself is another reason to visit. It's a charming mountain town with great restaurants, cozy cafes, and interesting shops. The town has a relaxed and friendly vibe, and it's a great place to come back to after a day of exploring the park. Whether you're looking for a nice meal, a warm cup of coffee, or just a comfortable place to stay, Banff town has it all. Plus, with the mountains all around you, the views from the town are always spectacular.

Banff is also a place where you can experience history and culture. The park has a rich Indigenous history, and there are several spots where you can learn about the local Indigenous peoples and their connection to the land. You can also visit historic sites like the Banff Springs Hotel, a beautiful old building that has been a landmark in the area for over a century.

One of the best things about Banff is that it's a place for everyone. Whether you're traveling alone, with friends, as a couple, or with family, Banff has something to offer. It's a place where you can have fun, relax, and make memories that will last a lifetime.

Banff is a great destination if you're looking for a place to feel inspired. There's something about being surrounded by such natural beauty that fills you with a sense of wonder and appreciation for the world around you. Whether you're watching the sunrise over the mountains or sitting by a lake, you can't help but feel connected to nature in a deep way.

Visiting Banff National Park is more than just a trip—it's an experience that will stay with you forever. From the breathtaking landscapes to the adventures you'll have, Banff is a place that will leave you feeling refreshed, inspired, and in awe of the natural world.

History and Cultural Overview

The history and culture of Banff National Park are as rich and fascinating as the landscapes that define it. This area has been a significant place for thousands of years, with its stunning mountains, lakes, and forests playing a vital role in the lives of Indigenous peoples.

Long before Banff became a national park, it was home to Indigenous groups such as the Stoney Nakoda, Blackfoot, and other First Nations. They have lived in this region for generations, relying on the land for their survival. The mountains and rivers were not just beautiful; they were part of their stories, traditions, and ways of life. These communities hunted, fished, and gathered food from the land, and their connection to nature was deep and spiritual. Today, you can still see the influence of these Indigenous cultures in the stories they share, the artwork displayed in local galleries, and the traditional practices that continue to thrive.

In the late 1800s, the area began to attract attention from outsiders. In 1883, three railway workers discovered hot springs in the region, which led to the establishment of the Banff Hot Springs. This discovery caught the interest of tourists, and soon, people began to visit to enjoy the natural hot springs and the breathtaking scenery. This influx of visitors prompted the Canadian government to recognize the need to protect the land, leading to the creation of Banff National Park in 1885. This made Banff the first national park in Canada and one of the first in the world.

As the park grew in popularity, so did the development around it. The town of Banff was established as a hub for tourists, with hotels, restaurants, and shops springing up to accommodate visitors. The iconic Banff Springs Hotel opened in 1888, becoming a symbol of luxury and hospitality in the area. This beautiful hotel, with its stunning architecture and breathtaking views, continues to be a popular destination for travelers from around the world.

Over the years, Banff National Park has become a cherished place for outdoor enthusiasts and nature lovers. It has also played a significant role in Canada's national identity, showcasing the beauty of the country's natural landscapes. The park is a symbol of conservation and a reminder of the importance of protecting the environment for future generations.

Today, Banff is not just a destination for adventure; it's also a place where history and culture are celebrated. Various cultural events, festivals, and art exhibitions take place throughout the year, highlighting the stories and traditions of the Indigenous peoples, as well as the cultural diversity that visitors bring. This blend of history, culture, and natural beauty makes Banff a unique and vibrant place to explore.

Visitors can learn about the Indigenous history of the area by visiting local cultural centers or joining guided tours that share stories of the land and its original inhabitants. These experiences offer valuable insights into the rich heritage of the region and help foster a deeper appreciation for its cultural significance.

Exploring the history and culture of Banff National Park is a journey that adds depth to your visit. Understanding the stories behind the stunning landscapes allows you to connect with the area in a more meaningful way. Whether you're hiking through the mountains, relaxing by a lake, or wandering through the charming town, you can feel the echoes of the past in the beauty that surrounds you. Embracing this history and culture will enhance your experience in Banff, making your visit even more memorable.

CHAPTER ONE
PLANNING YOUR TRIP

Best Time to Visit

Visiting Banff National Park is an experience that changes beautifully with each season. Each time of year brings its own charm and activities, making it a year-round destination for nature lovers and adventure seekers alike. Understanding what to expect in spring, summer, autumn, and winter will help you choose the best time for your visit.

Spring in Banff is a magical time as the snow begins to melt, revealing the lush greenery beneath. Expect temperatures to gradually rise, with daytime highs reaching around 10 to 15 degrees Celsius (50 to 59 degrees Fahrenheit). The landscape transforms into a vibrant tapestry of blooming wildflowers, fresh leaves, and rushing waterfalls. Iconic spots like Johnston Canyon come alive with thundering cascades, making it a perfect place for hiking. Wildlife also starts to emerge, so keep your eyes peeled for elk, deer, and even the occasional bear waking from hibernation.

Practical tips for spring include dressing in layers, as mornings can be chilly while afternoons warm up. A waterproof jacket is a must, especially if you plan to hike around waterfalls. Don't forget sturdy footwear for the trails.

One of the best activities in spring is the annual Banff Mountain Film and Book Festival, usually held in late April, showcasing incredible films and stories that celebrate mountain culture. This season is less crowded compared to summer, allowing for a more intimate experience with nature. Prices for accommodations are typically lower, making spring an appealing choice for budget-conscious travelers.

As you transition into summer, Banff bursts with life and color. Expect warmer weather with temperatures soaring up to 25 degrees Celsius (77 degrees Fahrenheit). The mountains are fully accessible, and the days are long and sunny. Lakes like Moraine Lake and Lake Louise shine in brilliant turquoise, perfect for kayaking or canoeing. The hiking trails range from easy walks to challenging climbs, with breathtaking views at every turn.

In terms of practical tips, packing sunscreen is essential, as the sun can be strong at higher elevations. A hat and sunglasses will help keep you comfortable during outdoor activities. Summer also brings plenty of events, including the Banff National Park Heritage Canada Day celebrations and music festivals.

However, summer is the peak tourist season, so expect larger crowds and higher prices for accommodations and activities. To navigate this, consider visiting popular sites early in the morning or late in the evening to avoid the busiest times.

Autumn casts a golden hue over Banff, making it one of the most picturesque seasons to visit. The temperatures start to cool, usually ranging from 5 to 15 degrees Celsius (41 to 59 degrees Fahrenheit). The trees turn brilliant shades of red, orange, and yellow, creating stunning landscapes perfect for photography. This is an excellent time for hiking, as trails are less crowded and the crisp air invigorates every step.

Practical tips for autumn include bringing layers to adjust to the cooler temperatures, especially in the mornings and evenings. A camera is a must for capturing the vibrant fall colors.

Autumn also features the Banff Jasper Collection's "Celebrate the Fall" events, which highlight local artists, food, and culture. The crowds start to thin out, leading to lower accommodation rates, making it a great time for those looking to enjoy the park without the hustle and bustle.

As winter blankets Banff in snow, the park transforms into a winter wonderland. Temperatures can drop to -10 degrees Celsius (14 degrees Fahrenheit) or lower, creating a serene and magical atmosphere. The iconic landscapes are perfect for snowshoeing, skiing, and ice skating on frozen lakes. The Banff Ski Resort becomes a hotspot for winter sports enthusiasts, with a variety of slopes catering to all skill levels.

Practical tips for winter include dressing in warm, waterproof clothing and investing in quality winter gear, including insulated boots, gloves, and hats to stay comfortable.

Winter festivals, such as the Banff SnowDays and Ice Magic Festival, celebrate the season with unique events and activities. The holiday season also brings a special charm to the town, with lights and decorations adding to the festive spirit. While winter is less crowded than summer, prices for accommodations can fluctuate, especially around holidays, so booking in advance is advisable.

When comparing the seasons, spring offers blossoming nature and fewer crowds, summer is vibrant with activity and energy, autumn captivates with breathtaking colors, and winter enchants with its serene beauty. Your choice of when to visit Banff will depend on what experiences you seek—whether you crave the warmth of summer sun or the quiet magic of winter snow. No matter the season, Banff National Park promises unforgettable memories in its stunning embrace.

How to Get There

Getting to Banff National Park is an exciting journey that opens up a world of stunning landscapes and outdoor adventures. The park is located in the heart of the Canadian Rockies in Alberta, and there are several ways to reach this incredible destination.

If you're flying in, the nearest major airport is Calgary International Airport, which is about 1.5 to 2 hours away from Banff. This airport has many domestic and international flights, making it convenient for travelers coming from various locations. Once you land, you can rent a car, which is a great option for exploring the area at your own pace. The drive from Calgary to Banff takes you through beautiful countryside and mountain scenery, making it a picturesque start to your adventure.

Another option is to take a shuttle service from the airport directly to Banff. Several companies offer this service, providing comfortable and hassle-free transportation. The shuttle ride typically takes about two hours, allowing you to relax and enjoy the views without the stress of driving.

If you prefer to travel by bus, there are several bus services that run from Calgary to Banff. These buses are affordable and convenient, often departing from the airport or downtown Calgary. The bus ride takes around 2 to 2.5 hours and is a great way to meet fellow travelers while enjoying the scenery.

For those who are already in Alberta, you can easily drive to Banff from nearby cities like Canmore or Jasper. The drive from Canmore is particularly short, taking just about 20 minutes, while the trip from Jasper will take you around 3 hours. The highways leading to Banff are well-maintained and offer breathtaking views of the mountains, forests, and rivers along the way.

Once you arrive in Banff, the town is compact and easy to navigate, with plenty of parking available for those who choose to drive. You can explore on foot, rent a bike, or use the local Roam public transit system, which provides convenient access to many popular attractions in and around the park.

If you're coming from further away, consider taking a road trip through the stunning Canadian Rockies. The scenery along the highways, particularly the Icefields Parkway, is breathtaking, with countless opportunities to stop and take photos of waterfalls, lakes, and wildlife. This iconic route is known for its jaw-dropping views and is often regarded as one of the most beautiful drives in the world.

In any case, whether you fly, drive, or take a bus, getting to Banff National Park is the first step in your adventure. Once you arrive, you'll be surrounded by incredible natural beauty, ready to explore all that this remarkable park has to offer.

Duration of your trip

Planning the duration of your trip to Banff National Park is essential for making the most of your time in this breathtaking area. The length of your stay can greatly influence the experiences you have and the activities you can enjoy, so it's important to consider what you want to do and see during your visit.

If you're looking for a quick getaway, a three-day trip can be quite fulfilling. This duration allows you to explore some of the park's main attractions without feeling rushed. You could spend your first day discovering the charming town of Banff, visiting the Banff National Park Museum, and taking a stroll along Banff Avenue to enjoy the local shops and restaurants. On the second day, a trip to Lake Louise is a must. You can hike around the lake, rent a canoe, or simply take in the stunning views. For the third day, consider a scenic drive along the Icefields Parkway, stopping at the breathtaking Peyto Lake and the Columbia Icefield. This will give you a taste of the natural wonders that define the park.

For a more in-depth experience, a week-long stay would allow you to delve deeper into the park's offerings. Within seven days, you can explore various hiking trails, visit different lakes, and even take part in activities like horseback riding or skiing, depending on the season. You could dedicate a couple of days to hiking iconic trails like the Plain of Six Glaciers or the Johnston Canyon, where the waterfalls are especially beautiful.

If you're an outdoor enthusiast or want to experience more of what Banff has to offer, extending your trip to ten days or even two weeks can provide a relaxed pace that allows for exploration. During this time, you can hike more remote trails, discover hidden gems like the less-visited Yoho National Park, or take part in guided tours, like wildlife watching or stargazing. This duration also allows for some downtime, where you can enjoy the hot springs or simply relax in nature.

Another thing to keep in mind is the time of year you visit. If you're traveling during the summer, the days are longer, which means you can fit in more activities. In contrast, winter days are shorter, but you can experience unique winter sports like skiing or snowshoeing. This seasonal difference might influence how you plan your days.

It's also a good idea to consider your travel style and personal preferences. Some people love a packed itinerary, while others prefer a slower pace to soak in the scenery. Whichever you choose, remember that Banff National Park offers a stunning backdrop that invites you to explore and enjoy every moment.

Whether you plan for a quick three-day visit or an extended stay of two weeks, the duration of your trip to Banff National Park should reflect your interests and the experiences you wish to have. This beautiful place has something for everyone, ensuring that you leave with unforgettable memories, no matter how long you stay.

Banff National Park on a budget

Exploring Banff National Park on a budget is not only possible but can also lead to a rich and fulfilling experience. With careful planning, you can enjoy the park's stunning beauty without breaking the bank.

Timing your visit is one of the most effective ways to maximize your budget savings. The shoulder seasons, which are late spring (May to early June) and early autumn (September to early October), offer some of the best opportunities for budget travelers. During these times, the crowds are thinner, and many accommodations lower their rates to attract visitors. You can enjoy the breathtaking scenery with fewer people around, making it easier to appreciate the peacefulness of nature. Additionally, some attractions may offer discounts during these periods, enhancing your overall experience.

When it comes to accommodation options, you have several budget-friendly choices. Hostels like HI Banff Alpine Centre are great for those looking to save money while still enjoying a comfortable stay. Prices can range from around $30 to $50 per night for a dormitory-style room. If you prefer a bit more privacy, guesthouses and bed-and-breakfasts like Banff International Hostel offer cozy accommodations, often starting around $80 per night. For those who enjoy cooking their own meals, consider vacation rentals or cabins available through platforms like Airbnb. These can vary widely in price, but you might find a decent place for $100 a night, especially if you book well in advance or during the off-peak seasons. Always keep an eye out for special deals or last-minute offers, which can lead to significant savings.

Activity planning is key to enjoying Banff without overspending. Many of the park's main attractions are either free or low-cost. For example, you can hike the trails around Lake Louise or Moraine Lake at no cost, taking in breathtaking views and immersing yourself in nature. The visitor centers often provide maps and information about self-guided tours that allow you to explore on your own. Keep an eye on local events, as festivals and markets frequently offer free activities and entertainment. The Banff Mountain Film Festival, for example, showcases breathtaking films that celebrate outdoor adventure, providing a great experience without a hefty price tag.

Dining on a budget in Banff can also be enjoyable. While many restaurants in the area can be pricey, there are affordable options available. Look for local eateries that offer hearty meals at reasonable prices, such as the Bear Street Tavern, where you can find delicious pizzas and salads for around $15. Another great option is the Bison Restaurant, which focuses on local ingredients and has items on the menu that won't break the bank. If you're feeling adventurous, consider trying street food or food trucks that often set up during the summer months. For a truly budget-friendly option, pack a picnic and grab supplies from the local grocery store or farmers' market. Eating outdoors surrounded by nature not only saves money but adds to the experience.

Transportation is another area where you can save money. If you're arriving in Banff, consider using a shuttle service from Calgary International Airport, which can be more affordable than renting a car. Once you're in the park, take advantage of the Roam Public Transit system, which offers convenient bus routes that connect various points of interest within Banff and Canmore. The cost is quite low, with fares around $2.50 per ride. Additionally, the Parks Canada Discovery Pass is worth considering if you plan to explore multiple parks. This pass covers entry to Banff National Park and many other locations for a flat fee, which can save you money if you visit more than once.

Enjoying a budget-friendly visit to Banff National Park is not only feasible but can also lead to incredible memories. By timing your visit wisely, choosing affordable accommodations, planning low-cost activities, and exploring budget dining options, you can experience the park's beauty and charm without overspending. With a little creativity and planning, you can find joy in the simple pleasures of nature and make the most of your adventure in this stunning destination.

Choosing the right tour package

Selecting the best tour packages for Banff National Park can greatly enhance your experience in this stunning destination. With a range of options available, it's important to understand the types of packages, what they offer, and how to choose the right one for your travel needs.

There are various types of tour packages that cater to different interests and preferences. Guided tours are popular for those who prefer an organized experience led by knowledgeable locals. These tours often include transportation, expert commentary, and access to special attractions. Self-guided walking tours provide flexibility for those who want to explore at their own pace. They usually come with detailed maps and information, allowing travelers to discover the park's beauty independently. Adventure excursions are perfect for thrill-seekers. These can include activities like white-water rafting, mountain biking, or wildlife safaris, often led by experienced guides who know the best spots to visit.

When considering the specifics of tour packages, the duration, cost, and inclusions can vary significantly. A typical guided day tour might last around 8 to 10 hours, with prices ranging from $100 to $200 per person, depending on the inclusions. Many of these packages include transportation, lunch, and stops at major attractions like Lake Louise and Moraine Lake. Self-guided tours can be more affordable, often priced between $50 to $100, and provide a great value as they usually include detailed maps and recommendations for trails. Adventure excursions can range widely in cost, from $150 for a half-day rafting trip to $400 for a full-day guided hike in more remote areas. It's essential to check what each package includes, as some may offer additional amenities like gear rental or park entrance fees.

Traveler suitability is another crucial factor in selecting the right tour package. Families might benefit from guided tours that cater to all ages, providing a comfortable way to explore with activities suitable for children. Couples may prefer more intimate experiences, such as sunset hikes or romantic dinner cruises on the lakes, which can create lasting memories. Solo adventurers may appreciate self-guided options that allow for personal reflection and exploration. For groups, adventure excursions can be a great way to bond over shared experiences, such as zip-lining or group hikes. Consider the interests and ages of your travel companions to find the best fit.

Seasonal considerations play a significant role in the availability and experience of tour packages. During the summer months, many guided tours and adventure activities are in full swing, offering the best variety and frequency. However, booking early is essential, as summer is the peak season. In contrast, winter offers unique opportunities for snowshoeing and ice skating, with fewer tourists. Some tours might be less available in the off-season, but this can also mean more personalized experiences and better pricing. The shoulder seasons, like late spring and early fall, can offer a balance of good weather, fewer crowds, and more affordable rates.

Local insights can add authenticity to your tour experience. Many travelers have enjoyed unique tours that aren't heavily advertised, such as a local wildlife photography tour led by experienced photographers who know the best spots for capturing the stunning landscapes and wildlife. Seeking recommendations from locals can lead to hidden gems that might not appear in typical travel guides. Engaging with local guides can also provide valuable tips on the best times to visit specific locations to avoid crowds or when to witness seasonal events like wildflower blooms.

When it comes to booking tips, it's important to do your research. Look for reputable tour operators with positive reviews on platforms like TripAdvisor or Google. Comparing different packages and their inclusions can help ensure you get the best value. Be wary of deals that seem too good to be true, as they may come with hidden costs or lower-quality experiences. If possible, book directly through the tour operator's website to avoid additional fees charged by third-party agencies. Early bookings can also secure better rates, especially during peak seasons.

Personalization and flexibility are key to crafting the ideal itinerary. Many tour operators offer customizable packages that can be tailored to your specific interests, whether that means combining different activities or adjusting the pace of your tour. For instance, you might consider booking a guided tour of the lakes and then adding on a self-guided hike in the afternoon. This combination can offer both structure and flexibility, allowing you to experience the park in a way that suits your style.

Choosing the right tour package for Banff National Park involves careful consideration of your interests, travel style, and the time of year. By researching various options, understanding the specific details of each package, and being open to local insights, you can select an experience that perfectly matches your needs. With thoughtful planning, your journey through Banff can be both memorable and enjoyable, providing a deeper connection to this breathtaking landscape.

Entry Fees and Park Passes

When planning a trip to Banff National Park, understanding entry and visa requirements is crucial for a smooth travel experience. The first step is determining whether you need a visa to enter Canada, as this can vary depending on your nationality and the length of your stay.

Visa requirements for Canada can be categorized into two main groups: travelers who need a visa to enter the country and those who require an Electronic Travel Authorization (eTA). Citizens from countries such as the United States, the United Kingdom, Australia, and most European Union nations typically do not need a visa for short stays, usually up to six months. Instead, they can travel with an eTA, which is a simpler and quicker process. On the other hand, travelers from countries like India, China, and several others must apply for a visa to enter Canada.

For those who need a visa, it's essential to understand the different types. The most common type for tourists is the Visitor Visa (Temporary Resident Visa), which allows entry into Canada for leisure purposes. If you plan to travel to Canada as part of a business trip or to visit family, there are specific visas for those purposes as well. For travelers heading to Europe before or after visiting Canada, it's worth noting the Schengen visa, which covers multiple European countries. Citizens from several countries, including the United States, Australia, and New Zealand, typically do not require this visa for short stays in Schengen countries.

The visa application process may seem daunting, but breaking it down into steps can make it more manageable. Start by checking the official Government of Canada website for visa requirements based on your nationality. This website provides comprehensive and up-to-date information tailored to your needs.

The following steps are involved in the visa application process:

1. Gather required documents: This typically includes a valid passport with at least six months of validity beyond your planned departure date, proof of travel arrangements (like flight bookings), accommodation details, and evidence of financial means to support your stay in Canada.
2. Complete the application form: You will need to fill out the appropriate application form, which is available online. Make sure to provide accurate information, as errors can lead to delays or rejections.
3. Pay the application fee: Fees can vary depending on the type of visa. Payment is usually made online during the application process.

4. Submit your application: You can submit your application online or at a local visa application center, depending on your country of residence.

5. Schedule an interview: In some cases, applicants may be required to attend an interview at a local consulate or embassy.

6. Wait for processing: Visa processing times can vary, so check the official website for estimates based on your nationality.

Practical tips can streamline this process. Start checking visa requirements well in advance of your travel date, ideally several months prior. This allows ample time to gather documents and complete the application. Utilize official resources, such as the Government of Canada's website or your local Canadian embassy, to ensure you have accurate and reliable information. Double-check that all your documentation is complete before submission to avoid delays.

Interactive elements, like checklists, can be helpful in tracking your progress. Create a simple checklist of required documents, application steps, and deadlines to keep everything organized. A flowchart could also guide you through the process of determining whether you need a visa or an eTA based on your nationality.

Example scenarios can illustrate how visa requirements may vary for different travelers. For instance, a traveler from the United States planning a week-long vacation in Banff would simply need to apply for an eTA online, requiring only a few basic documents and a small fee. In contrast, a traveler from

India might need to apply for a Visitor Visa, which could involve a more extensive documentation process, including proof of financial stability and an interview.

Navigating entry and visa requirements for Banff National Park involves understanding your nationality's visa needs and following a straightforward application process. By preparing well in advance, utilizing official resources, and staying organized, you can ensure a hassle-free experience as you embark on your adventure to one of Canada's most breathtaking destinations.

What to Pack for Every Season

Packing for Banff National Park can vary greatly depending on the season you choose to visit. Each season brings its own charm, and knowing what to bring will help you make the most of your trip.

In spring, temperatures begin to rise, but it can still be chilly, especially in the mornings and evenings. Expect a mix of sunny days and occasional rain. A lightweight jacket or a warm fleece is essential to keep you comfortable. Layering is key, so packing long-sleeve shirts and a good pair of hiking pants will serve you well. Waterproof shoes are a must, especially if you plan to hike on muddy trails. Don't forget your sunglasses and sunscreen, as the sun can be quite strong even in cooler weather. As for accessories, a hat can protect your face from the sun, and a reusable water bottle will keep you hydrated as you explore the beautiful landscapes.

Summer in Banff is warm and sunny, making it one of the best times for outdoor activities. Pack lightweight clothing like t-shirts, shorts, and breathable hiking pants. A good pair of hiking boots is important for tackling the trails, along with some comfortable sandals for relaxing after a long day of exploring. Don't forget to bring a hat and sunglasses to shield yourself from the sun. A light jacket or a sweater is wise for the cooler evenings. If you plan to camp or enjoy a picnic, pack a reusable cutlery set and a blanket. Always bring a refillable water bottle to stay hydrated, and consider packing snacks for your hikes.

Autumn brings stunning foliage and cooler temperatures, creating a beautiful backdrop for your visit. Packing layers is essential, as the weather can change quickly. Start with base layers like long-sleeve shirts and add a warm fleece or sweater. A waterproof jacket is great for unexpected rain, and sturdy hiking boots are essential for exploring the trails. Don't forget warm socks, as they can make a big difference on chilly hikes. A beanie or warm hat can help keep you cozy, along with gloves for those brisk mornings and evenings. As the days get shorter, packing a headlamp or flashlight can be useful if you plan on hiking later in the day.

Winter in Banff is a magical time, but it requires careful packing to stay warm and comfortable. Bring thermal base layers to keep your body heat in, along with insulated jackets and waterproof winter boots to handle the snow and ice. A good pair of gloves is essential, as are warm hats that cover your ears. Scarves can help protect your face from the cold wind. If you plan to ski or snowboard, don't forget your gear, or you can rent it when you arrive. For those who enjoy winter hiking, packing crampons for your boots can help navigate icy trails. Always carry a thermos with a warm drink and snacks to keep your energy up during your adventures.

What you pack for Banff National Park depends largely on the season. Being prepared with the right clothing and gear will not only keep you comfortable but also enhance your overall experience in this stunning natural wonder. Enjoy your adventure in Banff, no matter when you choose to visit.

CHAPTER TWO

GETTING TO BANFF NATIONAL PARK

Choosing the Best flights

Choosing the best flights to Banff National Park can make your travel experience much smoother and more enjoyable. To start, consider your departure city. If you are traveling from outside Canada, your primary airport options are Calgary International Airport, which is the closest major airport to Banff, or smaller regional airports. If you can, look for direct flights to Calgary, as they will save you time. However, if direct flights are not available, you might find good options with a stopover.

When booking your flight, it's important to compare prices. Use travel websites or apps to search for the best deals. Sometimes, booking directly through the airline's website can offer special promotions or better customer service if anything goes wrong. Be flexible with your travel dates if you can. Prices can vary greatly depending on the day of the week or time of year, so checking a few different dates can help you find a better deal.

Timing is also crucial. If you are planning to visit during peak seasons like summer or winter holidays, booking your flights well in advance is wise. This can help you secure lower fares and preferred flight times. Conversely, if you are traveling during the shoulder seasons, you may find more last-minute deals.

Consider the time of day for your flight. Morning flights are often less crowded and can sometimes be more affordable. Additionally, arriving in Calgary in the morning allows you to maximize your time in Banff since it's about a 90-minute drive from the airport.

Don't forget to check baggage policies and fees. Some airlines may offer lower fares but charge extra for checked luggage or seat selection. Knowing these details can help you budget for your trip better.

After booking your flight, keep an eye on your reservation. Sometimes airlines change flight times or gate assignments. It's good to stay informed to avoid any surprises on your travel day.

Consider travel insurance. While it may seem like an added expense, it can provide peace of mind if your flight gets canceled or if you have to change your plans unexpectedly.

By following these tips, you can choose the best flights that suit your needs and budget, ensuring a great start to your adventure in Banff National Park. Enjoy your journey!

Banff National Park airport: Arrival and Orientation

Arriving at Banff National Park starts with landing at Calgary International Airport, the main gateway for travelers heading to this beautiful region. Once you step off the plane, you'll find the airport is quite large but easy to navigate. After getting through customs and collecting your luggage, follow the signs to the ground transportation area where you can find various options to reach Banff.

One of the most popular choices is to rent a car. This gives you the freedom to explore the park at your own pace. Rental companies are located in the airport terminal, and you can book your car in advance online to ensure availability. Remember to check if your rental company has a good policy on mileage and fuel. The drive to Banff takes about 90 minutes, and the route is stunning, with mountain views and fresh air that will set the tone for your adventure.

If you prefer not to drive, there are shuttle services available that can take you directly to your hotel or to various points in Banff. These shuttles usually require a reservation, so it's a good idea to book in advance. Alternatively, taxis and ride-share services like Uber are also accessible at the airport for a more private journey.

Once you arrive in Banff, the town is compact and easy to navigate on foot. You can start your orientation at the Banff Visitor Centre, located in the heart of the town. The friendly staff there can provide you with maps, brochures, and the latest information on park activities and attractions. They can also help you with any questions you may have about your stay.

As you explore the town, you'll notice various shops, restaurants, and attractions. The main street, Banff Avenue, is lined with stores selling outdoor gear, souvenirs, and local crafts. You'll also find several places to eat, from casual cafes to fine dining restaurants, offering everything from hearty breakfasts to gourmet dinners.

Don't forget to check out local events happening during your visit. The town often hosts festivals, markets, and other activities that showcase the culture and community spirit of Banff. Keeping an eye on local calendars or asking at the Visitor Centre can help you find something fun to do.

If you plan to explore the national park itself, make sure you know the rules and regulations. The park is home to unique wildlife and stunning landscapes, so it's essential to follow guidelines for safety and conservation.

With your arrival at Calgary Airport and your first moments in Banff, you are beginning a journey filled with breathtaking nature, outdoor adventures, and unforgettable experiences. Enjoy every moment as you immerse yourself in the beauty of Banff National Park.

Journey to Banff National Park

The journey to Banff National Park is an exciting experience that sets the stage for your adventure in the heart of the Canadian Rockies. Whether you're traveling by car, shuttle, or bus, the route to Banff is as stunning as the destination itself.

If you arrive at Calgary International Airport, your journey begins here. After collecting your luggage and getting through customs, you can pick up a rental car if you plan to drive. Renting a car gives you the freedom to explore at your own pace and stop whenever you want to take photos or enjoy the views.

As you leave the airport, you will head onto the Trans-Canada Highway, also known as Highway 1. This highway is well-marked and leads directly to Banff. The drive takes about 90 minutes, but you may want to set aside a bit more time to soak in the scenery along the way.

The road winds through beautiful landscapes, with rolling hills, expansive fields, and majestic mountains coming into view. Keep your camera ready, as there are many opportunities to capture the stunning sights. The first glimpse of the Rocky Mountains will take your breath away, with their rugged peaks and the greenery of the forests below.

As you drive, you might see wildlife alongside the road. Keep an eye out for deer, elk, and even bears. However, it's essential to drive carefully and respect speed limits, especially in areas where animals may cross the road.

If you choose to take a shuttle or bus from the airport, the experience is equally enjoyable. Many shuttle services offer comfortable seating and scenic views along the way. These shuttles usually take the same route as cars and provide a great way to relax and enjoy the journey without worrying about navigation. You can sit back, enjoy the ride, and maybe even chat with fellow travelers who are just as excited about their visit to Banff.

Once you arrive in Banff, you will notice the charming town nestled among towering mountains. The first thing you may see is the iconic Banff Avenue, lined with shops, restaurants, and hotels. Take a moment to breathe in the fresh mountain air and let the beauty of your surroundings sink in.

As you start to explore, you'll feel the welcoming spirit of the town and the excitement of being so close to nature. Banff National Park is not just a destination; it's a place where adventure awaits at every turn, from hiking trails to stunning lakes.

Your journey to Banff National Park is just the beginning of an incredible experience. With its breathtaking landscapes, vibrant wildlife, and rich culture, Banff offers unforgettable moments that will stay with you long after your visit. Embrace the adventure and enjoy every step of the journey.

Train Options

Traveling to Banff National Park by train is a unique and enjoyable way to experience the beauty of the Canadian landscape. Trains offer a relaxing ride with stunning views, making the journey just as memorable as the destination.

If you start your journey in Calgary, one of the best options is to take the train to Banff with the Rocky Mountaineer or Via Rail. While the Rocky Mountaineer does not go directly to Banff, it offers an unforgettable journey through the Rockies, with some packages allowing you to combine the train experience with a bus transfer to Banff.

The Rocky Mountaineer is famous for its luxurious trains that provide exceptional service and comfort. This journey features large windows, gourmet meals, and knowledgeable guides who share stories about the region. The scenery along the way is breathtaking, showcasing mountains, rivers, and lush forests. Although this train ride can be pricey, many travelers find it worth the cost for the unique experience it offers.

Via Rail is another option, although it does not have a direct route to Banff. Instead, you can take a train from Calgary to Jasper, which is another beautiful area in the Canadian Rockies. From Jasper, you would then need to arrange a bus or shuttle to get to Banff. The Via Rail trains are comfortable and offer a chance to relax while enjoying the scenic views.

While traveling by train is a wonderful experience, it is essential to plan your journey in advance. Train schedules can vary, especially during peak travel seasons, so checking the timetable and booking your tickets early is a good idea. This ensures that you secure a seat and can choose the best times for your trip.

When you arrive in Banff, you will notice how accessible the town is from the train station. It's a short walk or a quick shuttle ride to get to the center of Banff, where you can start exploring the town and its many attractions.

Traveling by train to Banff National Park is a fantastic choice for those who appreciate scenic journeys and want to enjoy the beauty of the Canadian Rockies in comfort. Whether you choose the luxurious Rocky Mountaineer or the convenient Via Rail, you will create lasting memories on this special trip.

Bus Options

Traveling to Banff National Park by bus is a convenient and budget-friendly option that many visitors choose. Buses offer a comfortable way to reach this stunning destination while enjoying the beautiful landscapes along the way.

One of the most popular bus services is the Roam Public Transit, which connects Banff with Calgary International Airport and nearby towns. The Roam bus is reliable and affordable, making it an excellent choice for travelers. From Calgary, you can catch the Roam bus directly to Banff. The journey takes about one and a half to two hours, depending on traffic. The buses are comfortable, with large windows for enjoying the views, and they run frequently throughout the day.

Another option is to use shuttle services specifically designed for travelers heading to Banff. Companies like Sundog Tours and Brewster Express offer direct shuttle services from Calgary International Airport to Banff. These shuttles provide a hassle-free way to reach the park, often with a few scheduled stops along the way. The trip typically takes around two hours, and the shuttles are equipped with comfortable seating and luggage storage.

For those coming from other nearby cities, there are several bus companies that provide services to Banff. Greyhound used to offer routes to the area, but it's essential to check current schedules and availability as routes may change. Always check the bus company's website for the latest information on times and fares.

When planning your trip by bus, it's good to book your tickets in advance, especially during the busy summer months when many tourists visit Banff. Having your tickets ready will help you secure a spot and avoid any last-minute surprises.

Once you arrive in Banff, the bus station is conveniently located in the town center, making it easy to start your adventure. From there, you can explore the local shops, restaurants, and attractions on foot or catch a Roam bus to visit nearby sites within the national park.

Traveling by bus to Banff National Park is a practical choice for many visitors. It's an economical way to experience the beauty of the Canadian Rockies, allowing you to sit back, relax, and enjoy the scenery as you make your way to one of the most beautiful places in the world.

Any other travel option for Banff National Park

Banff National Park is a beautiful and enchanting place located in the heart of the Canadian Rockies in Alberta, Canada. This national park is known for its stunning landscapes, including towering mountains, sparkling lakes, and lush forests. The park covers over 6,600 square kilometers and is home to diverse wildlife, making it a paradise for nature lovers and outdoor enthusiasts.

One of the park's most famous features is Lake Louise, a breathtaking turquoise lake surrounded by high peaks and glaciers. The view of the lake, especially in the early morning when the water is calm, is nothing short of magical. Visitors can take leisurely strolls along the lakeshore or hike to one of the nearby viewpoints for a more panoramic view.

Another must-see in Banff National Park is Moraine Lake, often described as one of the most photographed lakes in the world. Its deep blue waters and the ten peaks of the Valley of the Ten Peaks make it a sight to behold. There are several hiking trails around the lake that cater to different skill levels, so everyone can enjoy the beauty of the area.

The town of Banff is also worth exploring. This charming town is full of shops, restaurants, and cafes, all nestled in a stunning mountain setting. The Banff Avenue is lined with beautiful buildings that reflect the area's rich history. Visitors can enjoy local cuisine, buy unique souvenirs, or relax in one of the many cafes while soaking in the views of the surrounding mountains.

For those who love adventure, Banff offers a wide range of outdoor activities throughout the year. In the summer, hiking, biking, and kayaking are popular ways to explore the park. There are trails for everyone, from easy walks to challenging hikes that lead to scenic vistas. Wildlife watching is another highlight, with chances to see elk, bears, and other animals in their natural habitat.

In the winter, the park transforms into a winter wonderland. Skiing and snowboarding at popular resorts like Sunshine Village and Lake Louise Ski Resort attract visitors from around the world. Snowshoeing and ice skating on frozen lakes are also enjoyable activities, providing a unique way to experience the snowy landscape.

Banff National Park is not just about the scenery and activities; it also has a rich cultural history. The area has been inhabited by Indigenous peoples for thousands of years, and visitors can learn about their traditions and connection to the land through various exhibits and guided tours.

Whether you are looking for adventure, relaxation, or a chance to connect with nature, Banff National Park has something for everyone. The stunning views, vibrant wildlife, and countless activities make it a perfect destination for all types of travelers. No matter when you visit, the beauty of Banff will leave you with unforgettable memories.

CHAPTER THREE

ACCOMMODATION OPTIONS

Luxury Hotel

Fairmont Banff Springs is an iconic hotel that resembles a grand castle nestled among the breathtaking mountains of Banff National Park. Located at 405 Spray Avenue, this stunning property is a blend of luxury and nature. When you arrive, you can feel the warmth and elegance of the place. The lobby is beautifully decorated, and the staff is incredibly welcoming. The hotel offers an array of activities to keep you busy. You can indulge in a soothing spa treatment, take a dip in the outdoor pool with views of the mountains, or enjoy fine dining at one of its exquisite restaurants. The hotel is also a great base for outdoor adventures. In the winter, you can easily access nearby ski resorts, while in the summer, hiking trails are just a short drive away. If you are on a budget, consider booking a room during the shoulder seasons when prices drop, or look for special packages that include meals or activities.

Next on the list is the Fairmont Château Lake Louise, located at 111 Lake Louise Drive. This hotel is famous for its stunning views of Lake Louise and the surrounding mountains. The moment you step inside, you are greeted by the breathtaking sight of the turquoise lake framed by towering peaks. You can spend your time here exploring the lake, hiking the scenic trails, or simply relaxing in the luxurious ambiance of the hotel. The dining options are exceptional, with restaurants offering everything from casual bites to gourmet meals. In winter, the lake transforms into a magical ice skating rink, and you can enjoy activities like snowshoeing or skiing nearby. For budget-conscious travelers, consider visiting during the off-peak season, when you might find more affordable rates, and don't forget to look for deals that include breakfast.

For those seeking a more rugged experience, camping in Banff National Park is a fantastic option. There are several campgrounds, like Tunnel Mountain Campground located at 10 Tunnel Mountain Road, where you can pitch a tent and immerse yourself in nature. The campgrounds are equipped with amenities like washrooms and picnic areas, making it a comfortable experience. You can spend your days hiking the trails, swimming in lakes, or simply enjoying the starry skies at night. Camping is a budget-friendly way to experience the park, and it allows you to connect with nature. Just remember to book your campsite in advance, especially during the busy summer months.

The Rimrock Resort Hotel, found at 300 Mountain Avenue, is another luxurious choice that offers breathtaking views and easy access to the park. This hotel is known for its exceptional service and fine dining experiences. The rooms are spacious and beautifully designed, providing a cozy retreat after a day of exploring. You can relax at the spa, dine at the award-winning restaurant, or take a short drive to nearby attractions like the Banff Gondola, which offers stunning views of the surrounding area. Travelers on a budget can check for seasonal discounts or packages that include meals or spa treatments, providing good value for your stay.

The Moose Hotel & Suites at 345 Banff Avenue offers a charming atmosphere with a touch of modern comfort. This hotel is a short walk from the heart of Banff, making it convenient for exploring local shops and restaurants. The Moose Hotel features comfortable rooms and suites, along with a rooftop hot tub that offers stunning mountain views. You can unwind in the cozy lounge or enjoy a meal at the on-site restaurant, which focuses on local ingredients. For budget travelers, it's a good idea to book in advance to secure the best rates and take advantage of any package deals that include breakfast or discounts for local attractions.

No matter where you choose to stay in Banff, there are countless ways to enjoy this magnificent destination while considering your budget. Exploring the natural beauty, dining on delicious local cuisine, and engaging in thrilling outdoor activities will create unforgettable memories in this stunning part of the world.

Budget-Friendly Hotel

Banff Park Lodge Resort Hotel & Conference Centre is a fantastic budget-friendly option located at 222 Lynx Street in Banff. This lodge offers comfortable accommodations and a variety of amenities, making it a great base for your adventures. The hotel has an indoor pool and a hot tub, perfect for unwinding after a day of exploring the stunning landscapes. The location is ideal, just a short walk from the heart of Banff, where you can find shops, restaurants, and attractions. You can easily venture out to nearby hiking trails, such as the Tunnel Mountain Trail, which offers spectacular views of the town and surrounding mountains. To save on your stay, consider booking directly through their website, especially during the shoulder seasons when prices tend to drop.

Next up is the Canmore Inn & Suites, situated at 1602 2 Avenue in Canmore, a charming town just outside Banff National Park. This hotel offers spacious rooms and a complimentary breakfast, making it a great choice for families or groups. The Canmore Inn is close to local attractions, including the Canmore Nordic Centre, where you can enjoy hiking and mountain biking trails in the warmer months. In winter, the area transforms into a playground for skiing and snowshoeing. The hotel also features an indoor pool, which is perfect for relaxing after a day outdoors. For budget-conscious travelers, booking a room with kitchen facilities allows you to prepare some of your meals, saving money during your stay.

Northwinds Hotel Canmore, located at 1602 2nd Avenue, is another excellent budget option. This hotel has a cozy atmosphere and offers easy access to outdoor activities. The rooms are clean and comfortable, providing a great space to rest after a day of adventures. One of the best things about Northwinds is its proximity to the downtown area, where you can explore local shops and enjoy delicious meals at affordable prices. Nearby, you can hike the Grassi Lakes Trail, known for its stunning turquoise waters and scenic views. Travelers on a budget should look for package deals that include breakfast, which can help save on food costs during your trip.

Bow View Lodge, found at 229 Bow Avenue in Banff, is a lovely spot for those wanting to experience the beauty of Banff without breaking the bank. The lodge has a charming rustic feel and offers fantastic views of the Bow River and surrounding mountains. It's a short walk to the downtown area, where you can enjoy local eateries and shops. You can also take advantage of the lodge's complimentary breakfast to kickstart your day. The nearby Bow River Pathway is perfect for leisurely strolls or bike rides along the river. For budget travelers, Bow View Lodge often runs promotions, so checking their website for deals is a smart way to save on your stay.

Samesun Banff is a vibrant hostel located at 433 Banff Avenue. This is a great choice for solo travelers or those looking to meet others on their journey. The atmosphere is friendly and welcoming, and the hostel offers both dormitory-style and private rooms at very reasonable rates. Samesun is just a short walk from downtown Banff, making it easy to explore the area. The hostel organizes activities, including hiking trips and social events, so you can connect with fellow travelers. The communal kitchen is a fantastic way to save money, allowing you to prepare your meals. When booking, keep an eye out for any special promotions or discounts that may be available.

Each of these budget-friendly hotels offers unique experiences while ensuring you have a comfortable stay in the beautiful surroundings of Banff National Park. By choosing wisely and planning ahead, you can enjoy a memorable trip without spending a fortune. Whether you're relaxing in a cozy lodge or mingling in a lively hostel, the beauty of Banff awaits you.

Mid-Range Hotel

Canmore Inn & Suites is a welcoming mid-range hotel located at 1602 2 Avenue in Canmore, just a short drive from Banff National Park. This hotel offers spacious rooms that come with comfortable beds and essential amenities, making it a great place to relax after a day of exploring. The location is excellent, as you can easily access the beautiful hiking trails surrounding Canmore, such as the Grassi Lakes Trail, which offers breathtaking views of turquoise waters and surrounding mountains. The hotel also provides a complimentary breakfast, which is a great way to save money on meals. For budget-savvy travelers, booking during the off-peak season can result in significant savings, so keep an eye out for those deals.

Next, the Coast Canmore Hotel & Conference Centre, situated at 511 Bow Valley Trail, provides a perfect blend of comfort and convenience. This hotel features cozy rooms, a lovely indoor pool, and a hot tub to help you unwind after a long day of activities. One of the highlights of staying here is the hotel's proximity to Canmore's vibrant downtown, where you can explore local shops and enjoy delightful dining options. For those looking to immerse themselves in outdoor activities, the Canmore Nordic Centre is nearby and offers fantastic trails for hiking and biking. The hotel often has special offers that include breakfast, which can help keep your travel budget in check.

Banff Park Lodge Resort Hotel & Conference Centre, located at 222 Lynx Street in Banff, is another excellent choice for mid-range accommodations. This hotel boasts comfortable rooms and a variety of amenities, including an indoor pool and a fitness center. Being just a short walk from the heart of Banff, it's easy to explore the charming streets filled with shops and restaurants. You can also take a stroll along the Bow River or venture to Tunnel Mountain for a hike that rewards you with stunning views of the surrounding area. To maximize your experience and save a little money, look for packages that include meals or special activities.

The Buffalo Mountain Lodge, at 700 Tunnel Mountain Road in Banff, offers a unique experience in a serene setting. This lodge features rustic-chic accommodations with a cozy atmosphere, making it feel like a true mountain retreat. The hotel is nestled among trees and offers easy access to hiking trails, including the popular Tunnel Mountain Trail. After a day of adventure, you can relax at the lodge's onsite restaurant, which serves delicious locally-sourced meals. For travelers on a budget, consider booking during the shoulder seasons when prices tend to drop and the crowds are thinner, allowing for a more peaceful experience.

The Rocky Mountain Lodge, located at 600 Spray Avenue in Banff, provides a delightful stay surrounded by nature. This lodge offers comfortable accommodations with a touch of rustic charm and beautiful mountain views. You'll find it easy to explore nearby attractions, including the stunning Banff Springs Golf Course and the picturesque Bow Falls. The lodge features amenities like a hot tub and a communal lounge area, where you can unwind after a day of exploring. Budget-conscious travelers should consider taking advantage of local transit options to get around and explore more of the surrounding areas without the cost of a rental car.

Choosing any of these mid-range hotels will enhance your experience in the breathtaking landscapes of Banff National Park and Canmore. Each place offers unique features and a welcoming atmosphere, ensuring that you enjoy your stay while keeping an eye on your budget. With careful planning and the right accommodations, your adventure in the Rockies can be both enjoyable and affordable.

CHAPTER FOUR
EXPLORING BANFF TOWN

Overview of Banff Townsite

Banff Townsite is a charming little town nestled in the heart of the Canadian Rockies, surrounded by stunning mountains and lush forests. As the first national park in Canada, Banff is rich in natural beauty and offers a perfect blend of outdoor adventures and cozy comforts. The town itself has a unique, picturesque vibe, with colorful buildings, quaint shops, and inviting restaurants lining the streets.

Walking around Banff, you'll find a variety of shops where you can buy everything from outdoor gear to souvenirs. The town has a welcoming atmosphere, making it easy to explore on foot. You can stroll along Banff Avenue, the main street, and take in the lovely mountain views at every turn. It's also home to many local artisans and craftspeople, so you can find unique handmade items that reflect the region's culture.

When it comes to dining, Banff has something for everyone. You can choose from casual cafes, family-friendly eateries, and upscale restaurants offering delicious meals made from fresh, local ingredients. Whether you're craving a quick bite or a multi-course dining experience, you'll find plenty of options that cater to your taste and budget.

In terms of activities, Banff Townsite serves as a great base for exploring the surrounding national park. You can easily access a range of outdoor adventures, from hiking and biking in the summer to skiing and snowboarding in the winter. The town is also home to beautiful parks, such as Central Park, where you can enjoy a leisurely picnic or just relax in nature.

One of the highlights of visiting Banff is the Banff Gondola, which takes you up Sulphur Mountain for breathtaking views of the surrounding landscape. Once at the top, you can enjoy walking along the boardwalk and taking in the panoramic sights of the Rockies. There's also the Banff Upper Hot Springs, where you can soak in warm, mineral-rich waters after a day of adventure.

Banff Townsite hosts various festivals and events throughout the year, showcasing local culture and celebrating the seasons.

From music festivals to winter carnivals, there's always something happening, making your visit even more enjoyable.

Getting around is easy, with plenty of public transportation options and walking paths throughout the town. If you're visiting during the summer, consider using the Roam transit system, which connects you to popular spots within Banff and even Lake Louise.

Banff Townsite is a delightful destination that combines natural beauty with a lively community. Whether you're an outdoor enthusiast or someone looking to relax and enjoy the scenery, this charming town has something for everyone. Exploring Banff Townsite is a wonderful way to immerse yourself in the beauty of the Canadian Rockies while enjoying the comfort and hospitality of the local community.

Top Attractions in Banff Town (Banff Avenue, Cave and Basin, Whyte Museum)

Banff Town is a treasure trove of stunning attractions that blend natural beauty with rich history and culture. As I strolled along Banff Avenue, explored the Cave and Basin, and visited the Whyte Museum, each experience left me in awe of this beautiful town.

Banff Avenue is the heart of the town, filled with vibrant shops, cafes, and restaurants. The moment I stepped onto the street, I was greeted by the stunning backdrop of the surrounding mountains. It's a wonderful place to spend time, whether you're window shopping or looking for unique souvenirs. The architecture is charming, with historic buildings that add to the town's character. I enjoyed stopping by local shops to browse handcrafted items and art inspired by the Rockies. There are also plenty of dining options, from cozy cafes to upscale eateries. I found a delightful little place for breakfast where I enjoyed freshly brewed coffee and a delicious breakfast burrito while soaking in the mountain views. Walking down the avenue is also a fantastic way to soak up the local vibe and meet fellow travelers who share your love for this stunning destination.

Cave and Basin National Historic Site, located at 311 Cave Ave, is another must-visit spot that tells the story of Banff's beginnings. To get there, it's just a short walk from the town center, and it's well marked. This historic site is where the hot springs were first discovered in 1883, leading to the establishment of Canada's first national park. As I wandered through the caves, I could feel the history surrounding me.

The interpretive center offers engaging exhibits that detail the natural history and cultural significance of the site. I took my time exploring the beautiful pools and enjoyed the serene atmosphere. The entrance fee is reasonable, and I felt it was well worth it for the experience. After my visit, I took a leisurely walk along the scenic paths outside, where the views of the surrounding mountains were simply breathtaking.

The Whyte Museum, located at 111 Bear St, is a cultural gem that showcases the art and history of the Banff area. It's an easy walk from Banff Avenue, and the museum itself is nestled in a lovely setting with beautiful gardens. As I entered the museum, I was greeted by warm, welcoming staff who were eager to share the stories behind the exhibits. The collections feature works by renowned artists and highlight the Indigenous cultures of the region. I was particularly drawn to the artwork depicting the breathtaking landscapes of the Rockies. The museum also hosts various events and workshops, making it a dynamic space that connects visitors with local culture. Entrance fees are modest, and I found it to be a worthwhile investment in understanding the rich tapestry of life in Banff.

During my time in Banff Town, I found that each attraction offered a unique glimpse into the area's history, culture, and stunning natural beauty. Whether I was enjoying a leisurely stroll along Banff Avenue, soaking in the history at Cave and Basin, or immersing myself in local art at the Whyte Museum, every moment was filled with wonder. The combination of breathtaking landscapes, engaging history, and vibrant culture made my visit truly unforgettable, and I recommend taking the time to explore these incredible attractions while soaking in the beauty of Banff.

Shopping, Dining, and Nightlife in Banff

Shopping, dining, and nightlife in Banff create a lively atmosphere that adds to the charm of this beautiful town. From unique boutiques to cozy restaurants and vibrant bars, there's something for everyone to enjoy.

When it comes to shopping, Banff offers a delightful mix of stores. Strolling down Banff Avenue, I discovered a variety of shops that cater to different tastes. There are outdoor gear stores where I found all the essentials for hiking and skiing. I loved browsing through the local art galleries that showcase stunning pieces by local artists, capturing the breathtaking beauty of the Rockies. I even stumbled upon charming souvenir shops, where I picked up some handmade crafts and unique gifts to remember my trip. If you're looking for something special, the boutiques have plenty of options, from stylish clothing to beautiful jewelry. Don't forget to take your time exploring; each store has its own unique flair, and you never know what treasures you might find.

Dining in Banff is a real treat, with a variety of options that cater to every palate. I started my culinary adventure at a local café, where I enjoyed a hearty breakfast of fluffy pancakes and fresh fruit. For lunch, I visited a casual eatery that offered delicious sandwiches and soups, perfect for fueling up after a morning of exploring. As the sun began to set, I found myself at a cozy restaurant with a view of the mountains, where I savored a delectable dinner of locally sourced ingredients. The atmosphere was warm and inviting, making it a perfect spot to relax and unwind after a day of adventure. For those looking for a quick bite, there are plenty of food trucks and casual spots that serve tasty meals on the go. Don't hesitate to ask locals for their favorite dining spots; they often have great recommendations that might not be on the tourist radar.

As the day transitions to night, Banff comes alive with a vibrant nightlife scene. There are several bars and pubs where you can enjoy a drink and socialize with fellow travelers. I found a lively pub that had live music, creating a fun and energetic atmosphere. The staff were friendly, and it was a great place to unwind with a local craft beer. If you prefer something quieter, there are wine bars and lounges that offer a more relaxed setting, perfect for enjoying a nice glass of wine or a creative cocktail. Some places even host trivia nights and special events, making it easy to meet new friends and enjoy a memorable evening.

Shopping, dining, and nightlife in Banff are experiences that enhance your visit to this stunning destination. Whether you're exploring local shops, savoring delicious meals, or enjoying a night out with friends, the charm of Banff is sure to leave you with wonderful memories. Embrace the local culture, try new foods, and take the time to enjoy everything this beautiful town has to offer.

CHAPTER 5.

ICONIC LANDMARKS AND SCENIC SPOTS

Lake Louise: The Jewel of the Rockies

Lake Louise, often referred to as the Jewel of the Rockies, is a breathtaking destination that captivates visitors with its stunning scenery and tranquil atmosphere. Nestled within Banff National Park in Alberta, Canada, this picturesque lake is famous for its turquoise waters, framed by majestic mountains and surrounded by lush forests.

Getting to Lake Louise is quite easy, and I found the journey to be part of the adventure. If you're driving, it's about a

45-minute trip from Banff townsite along the scenic Highway 1, also known as the Trans-Canada Highway. The drive itself is a feast for the eyes, with beautiful views at every turn. If you prefer not to drive, there are shuttle services that run from Banff to Lake Louise, making it convenient for those without a car. You can check the schedules online to plan your trip accordingly.

As I arrived at Lake Louise, the first sight of the lake took my breath away. The water sparkled in shades of blue and green, contrasting beautifully with the surrounding snow-capped peaks. It's no wonder this spot is so beloved. The iconic Fairmont Chateau Lake Louise sits right at the edge of the lake, providing a stunning backdrop. If you're feeling fancy, consider stopping in for a coffee or a meal at one of the restaurants there, as the views from the terrace are simply unforgettable.

One of the best ways to enjoy your time at Lake Louise is to take a stroll around the lake. There's a lovely walking path that circles the lake, and it offers different perspectives of the stunning scenery. I remember taking my time, snapping photos, and soaking in the serenity of the surroundings. The walk is suitable for all ages and abilities, making it a perfect outing for families, couples, or solo travelers. If you're up for a bit more adventure, you can hike up to the Lake Agnes Tea House, which is about a 3.5-kilometer hike from the lake. The tea house, nestled above the lake, offers a cozy spot to rest and enjoy some delicious snacks and teas.

In the summer, Lake Louise is a hub of activity. Kayaking and canoeing are popular, and you can rent a canoe right at the lake. Paddling out on the water provides a unique view of the towering mountains and is an experience I highly recommend. If you're visiting in the winter, the area transforms into a winter wonderland. You can go ice skating on the frozen lake or try your hand at snowshoeing or cross-country skiing on the nearby trails. The stunning views don't fade with the seasons; they only change, offering new adventures and experiences.

As the day comes to a close, the sunset over Lake Louise is a sight that stays with you long after you leave. The colors reflecting on the water create a magical atmosphere that is hard to describe. I suggest finding a quiet spot along the shore to take it all in.

If you're planning a visit, remember that Lake Louise can get busy, especially during peak tourist season. Arriving early in the morning can help you avoid crowds and give you the best experience. Whether you're seeking adventure, relaxation, or simply a moment of beauty, Lake Louise truly has it all. This magical place is a must-see when exploring the Rockies, and I guarantee that the memories you create here will last a lifetime.

Moraine Lake: The Valley of the Ten Peaks

Lake Louise, often referred to as the Jewel of the Rockies, is a breathtaking destination that captivates visitors with its stunning scenery and tranquil atmosphere. Nestled within Banff National Park in Alberta, Canada, this picturesque lake is famous for its turquoise waters, framed by majestic mountains and surrounded by lush forests.

Getting to Lake Louise is quite easy, and I found the journey to be part of the adventure. If you're driving, it's about a 45-minute trip from Banff townsite along the scenic Highway 1, also known as the Trans-Canada Highway. The drive itself is a feast for the eyes, with beautiful views at every turn. If you prefer not to drive, there are shuttle services that run from Banff to Lake Louise, making it convenient for those without a car. You can check the schedules online to plan your trip accordingly.

As I arrived at Lake Louise, the first sight of the lake took my breath away. The water sparkled in shades of blue and green, contrasting beautifully with the surrounding snow-capped peaks. It's no wonder this spot is so beloved. The iconic Fairmont Chateau Lake Louise sits right at the edge of the lake, providing a stunning backdrop. If you're feeling fancy, consider stopping in for a coffee or a meal at one of the restaurants there, as the views from the terrace are simply unforgettable.

One of the best ways to enjoy your time at Lake Louise is to take a stroll around the lake. There's a lovely walking path that circles the lake, and it offers different perspectives of the stunning scenery. I remember taking my time, snapping photos, and soaking in the serenity of the surroundings. The walk is suitable for all ages and abilities, making it a perfect outing for families, couples, or solo travelers. If you're up for a bit more adventure, you can hike up to the Lake Agnes Tea House, which is about a 3.5-kilometer hike from the lake. The tea house, nestled above the lake, offers a cozy spot to rest and enjoy some delicious snacks and teas.

In the summer, Lake Louise is a hub of activity. Kayaking and canoeing are popular, and you can rent a canoe right at the lake. Paddling out on the water provides a unique view of the towering mountains and is an experience I highly recommend. If you're visiting in the winter, the area transforms into a winter wonderland. You can go ice skating on the frozen lake or try your hand at snowshoeing or cross-country skiing on the nearby trails. The stunning views don't fade with the seasons; they only change, offering new adventures and experiences.

As the day comes to a close, the sunset over Lake Louise is a sight that stays with you long after you leave. The colors reflecting on the water create a magical atmosphere that is hard to describe. I suggest finding a quiet spot along the shore to take it all in.

If you're planning a visit, remember that Lake Louise can get busy, especially during peak tourist season. Arriving early in the morning can help you avoid crowds and give you the best experience. Whether you're seeking adventure, relaxation, or simply a moment of beauty, Lake Louise truly has it all. This magical place is a must-see when exploring the Rockies, and I guarantee that the memories you create here will last a lifetime.

Bow Valley Parkway and Bow Lake

The Bow Valley Parkway is a scenic route that runs through the heart of Banff National Park, connecting Banff to Lake Louise. This 48-kilometer drive is famous for its breathtaking views, abundant wildlife, and access to some of the area's most beautiful trails. I had the chance to experience this drive firsthand, and it was a journey filled with stunning landscapes and delightful surprises.

To get to the Bow Valley Parkway, you simply head west from Banff on Highway 1, and then take the exit for Highway 1A. The transition from the main highway to the parkway feels like stepping into a different world. As you drive, you'll find yourself surrounded by towering mountains, lush forests, and the sparkling waters of the Bow River. The road itself is well-maintained and offers plenty of pull-outs where you can stop and take in the scenery or snap some photos.

One of the highlights along the Bow Valley Parkway is Bow Lake, a stunning glacial lake that sits at the foot of the Crowfoot Mountain. The lake is about 30 kilometers from Banff and is easily accessible with parking available right by the shore. When I first laid eyes on Bow Lake, I was struck by its deep blue color, which looks almost surreal against the backdrop of the rugged mountains. The area is perfect for a picnic, and many visitors take the opportunity to relax on the shore while soaking in the views.

If you want to stretch your legs, there are several hiking trails around Bow Lake that are well worth exploring. One of my favorites was the short walk to the Bow Glacier Falls. This trail is about 4.5 kilometers round trip and takes you along the edge of the lake, offering spectacular views along the way. As I hiked, I could hear the sound of the rushing water from the falls in the distance, building my excitement for the view that awaited me. The trail was easy to navigate, making it suitable for families and casual hikers.

At the end of the trail, I was rewarded with a fantastic view of the Bow Glacier Falls cascading down the mountainside. The sight was breathtaking, and it felt incredible to be surrounded by such raw natural beauty. I spent some time there, just taking it all in and snapping pictures to capture the moment.

Another great stop along the Bow Valley Parkway is the famous Johnston Canyon. This spot is known for its stunning waterfalls and is a popular hiking destination. The hike to the Lower Falls is about 1.1 kilometers one way, and the Upper Falls is about 2.7 kilometers. The trails are well-marked, and the sound of the rushing water adds to the ambiance as you walk through the canyon. If you visit early in the morning or later in the afternoon, you can avoid the bigger crowds and enjoy a more peaceful experience.

As you continue along the Bow Valley Parkway, keep your eyes peeled for wildlife. It's common to see deer, elk, and even bears in the area, so be sure to have your camera ready. Just remember to maintain a safe distance and never approach wildlife. The beauty of this area lies not only in its landscapes but also in its vibrant ecosystem.

When planning your trip, I recommend visiting during the summer months for the best weather and accessibility. However, if you come in the fall, the changing leaves add a magical touch to the scenery. Whichever season you choose, make sure to bring plenty of water, snacks, and a camera to capture the unforgettable moments.

The Bow Valley Parkway and Bow Lake truly offer an enchanting experience that highlights the beauty of Canada's natural landscapes. Whether you're hiking, picnicking, or simply taking a scenic drive, this area is a must-visit for anyone exploring Banff National Park. It's a place where the beauty of nature surrounds you, and every turn offers something new to admire.

Johnston Canyon and Ink Pots

Johnston Canyon is one of the most popular destinations in Banff National Park, and for a good reason. This beautiful canyon is renowned for its stunning waterfalls, lush forest trails, and striking rock formations. I had the chance to explore this enchanting place, and it truly felt like stepping into a natural wonderland.

To get to Johnston Canyon, you start by driving along the Bow Valley Parkway. The address is Johnston Canyon, Lake Louise, AB T0L 1E0, Canada. It's about a 30-minute drive from the town of Banff, and the route is scenic and easy to navigate. There is a parking lot at the trailhead, but it can fill up quickly, especially during peak season. Arriving early in the morning is a smart move to secure a good parking spot and enjoy the trail before the crowds arrive.

As I set out on the trail, I was immediately struck by the beauty of the surrounding forest. The path is well-maintained and winds alongside the rushing waters of Johnston Creek. Along the way, you can hear the sound of the water flowing over rocks, which adds to the peaceful atmosphere. The trail to the Lower Falls is about 1.1 kilometers one way, making it an easy hike for families and casual walkers.

The first highlight of the hike is the Lower Falls. When I arrived, I was mesmerized by the sight of the water cascading down into a deep pool below. The view from the viewing platform is perfect for taking photos, and you can feel the cool mist on your face as the water splashes down. It's a great spot to take a moment and soak in the beauty of nature.

Continuing on to the Upper Falls requires a bit more effort, as the trail climbs higher and offers different perspectives of the canyon. The hike to the Upper Falls is about 2.7 kilometers one way, but it is well worth it. As I climbed higher, I could see the canyon walls getting steeper, and the views of the surrounding landscape opened up beautifully. When I finally reached the Upper Falls, I was greeted with another breathtaking view of the water plunging down from the rocky cliffs. It felt like a reward for my efforts.

If you're looking for a more extended adventure, I highly recommend continuing on to the Ink Pots after visiting Johnston Canyon. The Ink Pots are a series of stunning mineral springs located about 3.5 kilometers past the Upper Falls. The address for this area is also Johnston Canyon, Lake Louise, AB T0L 1E0, Canada. The trail to the Ink Pots is a bit more challenging but offers fantastic views of the mountains and valleys along the way.

As I hiked to the Ink Pots, the landscape changed from dense forest to wide-open meadows filled with wildflowers. The vibrant colors and fresh mountain air made the trek enjoyable. When I finally reached the Ink Pots, I was awestruck by the beauty of these clear blue-green springs, bubbling up from the ground. Each pool is unique in color, and the sight is mesmerizing. It felt like a hidden treasure tucked away in the mountains.

The Ink Pots are a lovely spot to take a break, have a picnic, and enjoy the tranquility of nature. It's a great place to relax and appreciate the beauty around you. I found a quiet spot to sit and enjoy my lunch, listening to the gentle sounds of nature and watching the clouds drift by.

For anyone planning a visit to Johnston Canyon and the Ink Pots, it's important to wear good hiking shoes and bring plenty of water and snacks. The trails can be uneven in places, and it's always a good idea to stay hydrated. If you're visiting in the summer, don't forget your sunscreen and a hat, as the sun can be strong.

Johnston Canyon and the Ink Pots offer a fantastic experience for anyone looking to connect with nature and witness some of the most stunning scenery in Banff National Park. Whether you're hiking to the falls, exploring the bubbling springs, or simply enjoying the peace of the forest, this area is a true gem that shouldn't be missed. It's a place where the beauty of the outdoors comes alive, and every step along the trail brings new wonders to discover.

Sulphur Mountain and Banff Gondola

Sulphur Mountain is one of the most iconic spots in Banff National Park, offering breathtaking views and a chance to connect with nature. My visit to Sulphur Mountain was truly memorable, and I can't wait to share my experience with you.

To get to Sulphur Mountain, you start by heading to the Banff Gondola base station. The address is 100 Mountain Ave, Banff, AB T1L 1B2, Canada. It's only about a five-minute drive from the town of Banff, making it easily accessible. If you prefer to walk, it's a pleasant 30-minute stroll from downtown along the Banff Avenue, which allows you to soak in the charming mountain scenery.

The Banff Gondola is a fantastic way to reach the summit of Sulphur Mountain. As you step into the gondola cabin, you can feel the excitement building. The gondola ride takes about eight minutes, during which you ascend over 700 meters to the summit. The views are absolutely stunning as you glide up the mountain, with the landscape stretching out beneath you. I found myself snapping photos of the breathtaking vistas the entire way up.

Once you reach the top, you step out onto the viewing platform, and it's like stepping into a postcard. The panoramic views of the Bow Valley and surrounding mountains are simply awe-inspiring. On a clear day, you can see all the way to the distant peaks of the Rockies. It's a great place to take a moment to breathe in the fresh mountain air and enjoy the beauty of nature.

The observation deck is well designed, allowing visitors to take in the scenery from various angles. There are informative signs that explain the geography and history of the area, making it a great spot for learning while you enjoy the views. I spent a good amount of time here, just soaking it all in and appreciating the spectacular sights.

For those wanting to explore more, there are several walking trails at the summit. The Sulphur Mountain Boardwalk is a must-do. This easy, 1-kilometer wooden boardwalk winds its way along the ridge and offers incredible views of the surrounding area. Walking along the boardwalk, I felt like I was on top of the world, surrounded by the majestic peaks of the Rockies. The boardwalk leads to the historic Cosmic Ray Station, where you can learn more about the scientific research that has taken place on the mountain.

If you're feeling adventurous, you can also hike down the mountain instead of taking the gondola back. The hike to the base is about 5.5 kilometers and offers a different perspective of the scenery. I decided to hike back down, and it was an excellent decision. The trail is well-marked and gives you a chance to appreciate the flora and fauna up close. I spotted some lovely wildflowers along the way and even saw a few friendly chipmunks.

When planning your visit, it's a good idea to check the weather. The views can change dramatically with the weather conditions, and clear skies will give you the best experience. Also, consider purchasing your gondola tickets in advance, especially during peak season, to avoid long waits.

The Banff Gondola and Sulphur Mountain are not just about the breathtaking views; they also offer a fantastic opportunity to connect with the beauty of nature. Whether you take the gondola to the top, hike the trails, or just relax and enjoy the scenery, Sulphur Mountain is a highlight of any trip to Banff. It's a place that truly showcases the magic of the Rockies and leaves you with unforgettable memories.

CHAPTER SIX

HIKING AND OUTDOOR ADVENTURES

Best Hikes for Beginners (Tunnel Mountain, Fenland Trail)

If you're new to hiking and looking for some great beginner trails in Banff, Tunnel Mountain and the Fenland Trail are perfect choices. Each offers its own unique scenery and experience, making them wonderful options for anyone wanting to explore the beauty of the area.

Let's start with Tunnel Mountain. The address to the trailhead is Tunnel Mountain Dr, Banff, AB T1L 1A1, Canada. It's just a short drive or a nice walk from downtown Banff, which makes it super convenient. If you're walking from the town, it takes about 20 to 30 minutes, and you'll enjoy the fresh mountain air as you approach the trailhead.

The Tunnel Mountain hike is about 4.5 kilometers (round trip) and takes roughly one to two hours to complete, depending on your pace. As you start the hike, you'll find the trail well-marked and easy to follow. The first part of the trail is a bit steep, but it's manageable for beginners. I remember feeling excited as I began my ascent, knowing that a fantastic view awaited me at the top.

Along the way, there are several spots to pause and catch your breath while taking in the surrounding beauty. The trail winds through beautiful trees and offers glimpses of the Bow Valley as you climb. As I hiked, I enjoyed the sounds of nature—birds chirping and leaves rustling in the gentle breeze. After a bit of effort, I finally reached the summit, and wow, what a reward! The panoramic view of Banff and the surrounding mountains was absolutely breathtaking. It felt like a moment of triumph, standing there with the world sprawled out below me.

Once you've soaked in the views, take your time enjoying the peaceful atmosphere at the top. It's a fantastic spot for photos or simply relaxing before heading back down. The hike back is much easier, allowing you to appreciate the landscape in a different light.

Now, let's talk about the Fenland Trail. This trail is located at the Fenland Trailhead, just off the Bow Valley Parkway, with the address being 2-2040, Banff, AB T1L 1A1, Canada. The Fenland Trail is also very accessible, and it's a beautiful walk that takes you through a lovely forest and along the banks of the Bow River.

The Fenland Trail is a 2-kilometer loop, making it perfect for a leisurely stroll. The trail is flat and wide, which is great for beginners or families. Getting there from Banff is easy; it's about a five-minute drive, or you can cycle there if you're feeling adventurous. There are plenty of parking spots available if you're driving.

As you walk along the Fenland Trail, you'll be surrounded by the sounds of nature. The trees provide a lovely canopy overhead, and you might spot some local wildlife, like squirrels or birds. The trail is marked with information signs, so you can learn about the area's flora and fauna as you go. I loved stopping to read these signs and discovering new things about the environment around me.

The Fenland Trail eventually leads to a picturesque viewpoint along the Bow River. Here, you can sit on a bench and enjoy the sight of the water flowing gently by, with the mountains framing the background. It's a peaceful spot that invites you to linger a little longer, soaking in the beauty of nature. Whether you're enjoying a picnic or just taking a moment to breathe in the fresh air, it's a wonderful place to unwind.

Both of these hikes are fantastic options for beginners. They provide opportunities to experience the stunning landscapes of Banff without requiring extensive hiking experience. As you explore Tunnel Mountain and the Fenland Trail, you'll find joy in the simple pleasures of nature. Don't forget to bring water, wear comfortable shoes, and take your time enjoying the journey. With these hikes, you'll leave with memories and perhaps even a newfound love for the outdoors.

Moderate Hikes (Larch Valley, Lake Agnes Tea House)

For those looking for a moderate hiking experience in the breathtaking scenery of Banff National Park, the Larch Valley and Lake Agnes Tea House hikes are two fantastic options. Each trail offers stunning views and a chance to experience the beauty of the Canadian Rockies.

Let's start with Larch Valley. The trailhead is located at Moraine Lake, which has the address Moraine Lake Rd, Lake Louise, AB T0L 1E0, Canada. To get there, you can drive from Banff, which takes about 45 minutes. Keep in mind that parking can fill up quickly, especially during the summer months, so arriving early is a good idea. If the parking lot is full, shuttle services are available from the Lake Louise area, making it easier to reach the lake.

The Larch Valley trail is around 7 kilometers (about 4.4 miles) round trip, and it generally takes about three to four hours to complete. The hike begins by winding through a stunning forest of pine trees, with the sound of the wind rustling through the branches adding to the peaceful atmosphere. As you climb, the scenery opens up to reveal beautiful views of Moraine Lake below, with its striking turquoise waters surrounded by towering peaks.

As you approach the valley, the path becomes a bit steeper, but the effort is well worth it. When I reached the Larch Valley, I was greeted by a breathtaking sight. The vibrant golden larch trees in the fall create a stunning contrast against the rocky backdrop of the mountains. This area is known for its beautiful autumn foliage, making it a perfect time to visit if you enjoy colorful landscapes. I remember taking countless photos, trying to capture the beauty around me, but it felt even better to simply stand there and soak it all in.

At the top, there are several options for further exploration. You can continue your hike up to Sentinel Pass for even more spectacular views or simply relax and enjoy a picnic surrounded by nature. It's a great spot to recharge before heading back down. The return hike allows you to appreciate the changing perspectives of the landscape, making the journey back just as enjoyable.

Now, let's move on to the Lake Agnes Tea House hike. The trailhead is also located at the Lake Louise area, and you can find it at the address Lake Agnes Trail, Lake Louise, AB T0L 1E0, Canada. This hike is another favorite, as it leads you to the charming Lake Agnes and the historic tea house perched on its shores.

To get to the trailhead, you can park at the Lake Louise parking lot and start from there. It's important to arrive early, as the parking area can fill up fast, especially during peak tourist seasons. Once on the trail, the hike is about 7 kilometers (around 4.4 miles) round trip, with an elevation gain of around 400 meters. The hike generally takes around two to three hours, depending on your pace.

As you walk, you'll find the trail well-maintained and easy to follow. The path leads you through a lush forest with beautiful views of the surrounding mountains. Along the way, I encountered friendly hikers who were just as excited about the journey. The trail has a few steeper sections, but the views are so captivating that you won't mind pausing to catch your breath.

When I finally reached Lake Agnes, I was struck by its serene beauty. The water is crystal clear, and the mountains reflect off its surface, creating a picture-perfect scene. The tea house is just a short walk away from the lake, and stepping inside is like entering a cozy, welcoming haven. It's the perfect spot to take a break, enjoy a cup of tea, and indulge in some freshly baked treats. I remember sitting on the patio, surrounded by fellow hikers, all enjoying the views and sharing stories of their adventures.

After enjoying the tea house, take some time to explore the area around Lake Agnes. You can sit on the shore and appreciate the tranquility, or take a short walk around the lake for different perspectives of the stunning scenery. If you're feeling adventurous, consider continuing on to the Big Beehive, which offers even more spectacular views of the area.

Both Larch Valley and Lake Agnes Tea House hikes are perfect for those looking to challenge themselves a bit while still being able to enjoy the beauty of the Canadian Rockies. With stunning landscapes and the opportunity to connect with nature, these trails are sure to leave you with unforgettable memories. Remember to bring plenty of water, wear comfortable hiking shoes, and take your time to truly enjoy everything the hikes have to offer.

Challenging Treks (Plain of Six Glaciers, Sentinel Pass)

For those seeking an adventurous challenge in the stunning landscapes of Banff National Park, the Plain of Six Glaciers and Sentinel Pass hikes are fantastic options. Both treks offer breathtaking views, a chance to see glaciers up close, and a rewarding experience that will stay with you long after your trip.

Let's begin with the Plain of Six Glaciers hike. The trailhead is located at Lake Louise, which you can find at the address Lake Louise, AB T0L 1E0, Canada. Getting there is straightforward; simply drive to the Lake Louise area, which is about a 45-minute drive from Banff. Be aware that parking can fill up quickly, especially in the summer, so it's wise to arrive early or consider taking a shuttle from the Banff area.

The hike to the Plain of Six Glaciers is about 14 kilometers (approximately 8.7 miles) round trip, and it usually takes about five to six hours to complete. The trail begins at the same spot as the Lake Agnes hike, so you'll already be familiar with the beautiful surroundings. As you start your journey, the path winds through a lush forest, filled with the sounds of nature, including birds chirping and the gentle rustle of leaves.

As you ascend, the trail opens up to stunning views of Lake Louise and the surrounding mountains. The first stretch is relatively moderate, but as you get closer to the glaciers, the trail becomes steeper and more challenging. I remember pushing myself up the rocky path, feeling a mix of exhilaration and fatigue, but every step brought me closer to an incredible sight.

When I finally reached the Plain of Six Glaciers, I was awestruck. The glaciers towered above me, glistening in the sunlight, and the entire area felt untouched by time. This spot is ideal for taking in the vastness of the landscape, snapping photos, and enjoying the peacefulness that surrounds you. The view is nothing short of spectacular, and it's hard to capture the sheer beauty in words.

At the top, you'll find a small teahouse, which is a great place to take a break. Enjoy a hot drink while taking in the view, and don't forget to refuel with some snacks. After resting, consider exploring the area further. You can hike closer to the glaciers or simply find a quiet spot to sit and soak in the stunning scenery before heading back down.

Now, let's move on to the Sentinel Pass hike. This trail also starts from the Lake Louise area, specifically at the Lake Louise parking lot, located at the same address, Lake Louise, AB ToL 1Eo, Canada. The Sentinel Pass trail is about 10 kilometers (approximately 6.2 miles) round trip, with a challenging elevation gain of about 700 meters. It typically takes about four to five hours to complete the hike.

As you set off on this trail, you'll initially follow the same route as the Plain of Six Glaciers hike before branching off. The path begins with a beautiful forested area, where you might spot some wildlife, such as squirrels or even deer. After about a kilometer, the trail starts to climb, and you'll be treated to spectacular views of the surrounding mountains and valleys.

The hike to Sentinel Pass is steep, but the rewarding views make it all worthwhile. As you near the pass, the terrain becomes rocky, and you'll feel the burn in your legs, but keep going! I vividly recall reaching the top, where I was greeted with one of the most breathtaking views I've ever seen. From the pass, you can see down into the Valley of the Ten Peaks, and the sight is simply mesmerizing.

Take your time at the top to enjoy the view and have a snack. It's a perfect spot to reflect on your journey and appreciate the beauty of nature. If you're up for more adventure, you can continue on to hike the trail that leads to the upper section of the valley for even more stunning panoramas.

Both the Plain of Six Glaciers and Sentinel Pass hikes are perfect for those looking to challenge themselves while experiencing the stunning beauty of Banff National Park. Each trek offers a unique perspective of the incredible landscapes, from glaciers to mountain vistas. Be sure to wear sturdy hiking boots, carry plenty of water, and bring snacks to keep your energy up. Remember to take your time, enjoy the journey, and soak in all the beauty around you. These hikes are not just about the destination; they're about the adventure and the memories you create along the way.

Wildlife Safety Tips and Hiking Etiquette

Exploring the breathtaking landscapes of Banff National Park offers incredible opportunities to encounter wildlife. However, it's essential to keep safety in mind and understand the etiquette that ensures a respectful and enjoyable experience for everyone, including the animals.

Wildlife safety is crucial when hiking in areas like Banff. The park is home to various animals, including bears, elk, moose, and mountain goats. Before heading out, it's wise to educate yourself about these creatures and how to behave if you encounter them. Always start your journey at a trailhead, which is often well-marked and easy to find. For example, you can begin your hike at the Bow Valley Parkway trailhead located at 1A Highway, Banff, AB ToL oCo, Canada.

When hiking, it's best to go in groups. Animals are less likely to approach a larger group of people. Making noise while you walk, like talking or singing, can help alert wildlife to your presence, giving them a chance to move away. I remember hiking with friends and keeping our voices lively; it felt natural and helped us feel safer.

If you do encounter wildlife, keep a respectful distance. For bears, the general rule is to stay at least 100 meters (about 328 feet) away. If you spot a bear, don't run. Instead, back away slowly while keeping your eyes on the animal. I once saw a black bear from a distance while hiking, and I felt a rush of excitement but knew to stay calm and collected.

If a bear or any large animal approaches you, make yourself appear larger by raising your arms or holding your backpack above your head. If you feel threatened, use bear spray if you have it, and shout firmly to assert your presence. It's a good idea to carry bear spray in a holster for quick access. Knowing how to use it beforehand can be life-saving.

When it comes to hiking etiquette, always stay on marked trails. Not only does this protect the delicate environment, but it also minimizes the chances of surprising wildlife. Observing the rules about trail use helps preserve the natural beauty for future visitors. I remember walking on established paths and enjoying the vibrant wildflowers and clear streams, feeling good that I was contributing to their protection.

If you're hiking during the spring or fall, be especially cautious, as animals may be more active during these times. For instance, elk are often seen near the roads in the fall, and they can become aggressive if they feel threatened. During my visit in the autumn, I was amazed to see a herd of elk grazing peacefully, but I made sure to keep my distance and appreciate them from afar.

Always carry enough water and snacks to keep your energy up during your hike. Hydration is key, especially when you're out in the sun for hours. I always pack my favorite trail mix and keep a bottle of water handy. It's important to take breaks, enjoy the scenery, and share stories with friends about the wildlife we might encounter.

Also, consider the Leave No Trace principles. Pack out everything you bring with you, including food wrappers and other waste. Respecting the environment shows that you care for the place you love to explore. I always take pride in ensuring I leave the trails as I found them, which adds to the enjoyment of hiking.

Exploring the incredible wildlife of Banff National Park is a thrilling experience, but it comes with responsibilities. By prioritizing safety and practicing good hiking etiquette, you can ensure a memorable adventure for yourself and the wildlife you encounter. Remember to stay calm, be respectful, and enjoy the majestic beauty that surrounds you. Every hike can be an unforgettable journey, filled with the wonders of nature if we approach it thoughtfully.

Water Adventures

Banff National Park is not just about majestic mountains and stunning trails; it's also a paradise for water adventures. Whether you're gliding across serene lakes, braving whitewater rapids, or simply relaxing in hot springs, there's something for everyone. Let me take you through some of the best water activities to enjoy in and around Banff.

Canoeing and kayaking on the lakes is a fantastic way to experience the beauty of the park. One of the most popular spots is Lake Louise, located at 501 Lake Louise Dr, Lake Louise, AB T0L 1E0, Canada. The lake's turquoise waters are surrounded by towering peaks and lush forests, making it a breathtaking place to paddle. You can rent a canoe right at the boathouse during the summer months. It's such a peaceful experience to glide across the water, listening to the gentle lapping of waves while soaking in the stunning scenery. I remember my first time on Lake Louise; the reflections of the mountains in the water were mesmerizing, and I felt a deep connection to nature. If you're feeling adventurous, bring a kayak for a more personal experience on the water.

Another great location for canoeing and kayaking is Moraine Lake, which is about 14 kilometers from Lake Louise. To get there, take the Moraine Lake Road (this road is only open seasonally), and parking fills up quickly, so it's best to arrive early. The vibrant blue color of the water against the backdrop of the Valley of the Ten Peaks is something you have to see to believe. When I visited, I felt like I was in a postcard. Make sure to explore the shoreline and take lots of pictures!

If you're looking for something more thrilling, consider whitewater rafting on the Kicking Horse River. This river is famous for its exciting rapids, making it a perfect spot for adventure seekers. The closest rafting company is Kicking Horse River Rafting, located at 221 6 St, Golden, BC V0A 1H0, Canada. It's about an hour's drive from Banff, and the drive itself offers beautiful mountain views. Many companies offer guided tours, which are great for both beginners and experienced rafters. I joined a guided trip and found it exhilarating to navigate the rapids, all while surrounded by spectacular landscapes. The guides were fantastic, providing safety instructions and sharing interesting facts about the area.

For those who enjoy fishing, Banff offers fantastic opportunities for angling. The Bow River is known for its abundance of trout, and you can find several spots ideal for fishing, such as the area near the Bow River Bridge, located off Bow River Ave, Banff, AB T1L 1H8, Canada. You'll need a fishing license, which you can easily purchase online or at local shops. Spending a quiet morning fishing while listening to the sounds of nature is one of the best ways to unwind. I remember sitting by the river, casting my line, and enjoying the peaceful surroundings. If you're not a pro at fishing, there are guided tours available that can provide you with all the necessary equipment and tips.

Swimming in Banff is a delightful experience, especially when you consider the hot springs and natural pools available. The Banff Upper Hot Springs, located at 1 Mountain Ave, Banff, AB T1L 1K2, Canada, is a perfect place to relax after a day of adventures. The hot springs have been enjoyed for over a century and offer stunning views of the surrounding mountains. The water is warm and soothing, making it a great spot to soak and unwind. I loved sinking into the warm water after a long hike, feeling my muscles relax while gazing at the stars above.

For a more natural swimming experience, head to Johnson Lake, which is about a 15-minute drive from the Banff townsite. The lake is located off of Johnson Lake Rd, Banff, AB T1L 1C1, Canada. The clear water is perfect for a refreshing dip, and there are picnic areas nearby to enjoy lunch after swimming. I enjoyed spending a sunny afternoon there, swimming, and watching the playful kids splashing around while their parents relaxed on the shore.

The water adventures in and around Banff National Park are simply unforgettable. Whether you're canoeing across crystal-clear lakes, rafting through exhilarating rapids, casting a line in the Bow River, or soaking in hot springs, there's something for everyone to enjoy. These activities provide unique ways to connect with nature, and each moment is an opportunity to create lasting memories. Don't forget to pack your swimsuit, sunscreen, and a sense of adventure, and you'll be ready for an incredible time in this beautiful part of Canada.

CHAPTER 7.

WILDLIFE BANFF NATIONAL PARK

Overview of Wildlife Species (Bears, Elk, Wolves)

Banff National Park is a stunning place not just for its breathtaking landscapes but also for its diverse wildlife. As you explore the park, you might encounter some amazing animals that call this area home. Let me share with you an overview of some of the most iconic wildlife species you can see in Banff, including bears, elk, and wolves.

Bears are perhaps the most famous residents of Banff National Park. Both black bears and grizzly bears roam these mountains and forests. Black bears are generally smaller and have a sleek, black coat, while grizzly bears are larger with a distinctive hump on their back and a brownish color. Seeing a bear in the wild can be an unforgettable experience, but it's important to keep your distance. If you're lucky enough to spot one, remember to stay at least 100 meters away. You can often see bears foraging for berries in the summer months or roaming through the woods. I once saw a mother bear with her cubs near the Bow Valley Parkway, and it was heartwarming to watch them play and interact. Just make sure to keep your food secured and follow safety guidelines to avoid any encounters.

Elk are another magnificent species that can be found in Banff. These large mammals have impressive antlers, especially the males, and they often roam through meadows and forests. The best time to see elk is during the early morning or late afternoon when they are most active. I remember walking around the town of Banff and coming across a group of elk grazing peacefully in the grass. It was fascinating to see them up close, and their gentle demeanor makes them a favorite among visitors. Just be cautious, as they can be unpredictable, especially during the rutting season in the fall when males are more aggressive.

Wolves are among the most elusive creatures in Banff National Park. They play a vital role in maintaining the balance of the ecosystem. Though they are not often seen, there are wolf packs that inhabit the area. If you are lucky, you might catch a glimpse of them during your hikes or while driving along certain park roads. Wolves are known for their howling, and if you listen closely, you might hear them communicating with each other, especially at dawn or dusk. I remember sitting quietly one evening and hearing a distant howl echo through the mountains, which gave me chills and a sense of connection to nature.

When exploring the park, it's important to respect wildlife and their habitat. Always stay on marked trails, keep your distance from animals, and never feed them. This helps ensure that the wildlife remains wild and safe for everyone to enjoy.

Banff National Park is home to a rich variety of wildlife, including bears, elk, and wolves. Each species offers a unique glimpse into the beauty of nature. Whether you're hiking through the forest, driving along scenic routes, or just enjoying the views, keep your eyes open for these incredible animals. Witnessing them in their natural habitat is a rewarding experience that adds to the magic of your visit to this stunning national park.

Best Wildlife Viewing Areas

Banff National Park is a wildlife lover's paradise, offering some of the best spots to see animals in their natural habitat. Whether you're hoping to catch a glimpse of majestic elk, playful bears, or elusive wolves, there are several prime locations in the park where you're likely to have an unforgettable experience.

One of the best places for wildlife viewing is the Bow Valley Parkway. This scenic drive runs parallel to the Bow River and is surrounded by stunning mountains and lush forests. As you drive along this road, keep your eyes peeled for bears, particularly in the spring and early summer when they emerge from hibernation. I once saw a black bear foraging for berries right off the roadside. The parkway is also a great spot to see elk grazing in the meadows, especially near the entrances of the park.

Another fantastic location is the Lake Minnewanka area. This large glacial lake is surrounded by beautiful mountains and offers excellent opportunities for wildlife viewing. The area is known for its bighorn sheep, which can often be seen along the rocky slopes. The lake itself is a serene spot for picnicking or just relaxing while you wait for wildlife to appear. I remember sitting by the shore and watching a group of sheep navigate the rocky terrain—it was a breathtaking sight.

If you're up for a hike, consider the Johnston Canyon trail. This popular trail takes you through beautiful scenery and leads to stunning waterfalls. Along the way, keep an eye out for various bird species and, if you're lucky, you might even spot a bear or elk. The trail can get busy, especially in the summer, but the wildlife sightings make the journey worthwhile. The sounds of the waterfalls combined with the possibility of seeing animals create a magical atmosphere.

The area around Vermilion Lakes is also a great choice for wildlife viewing. This wetland area is home to many species of birds, including herons, ducks, and even the occasional osprey. I enjoyed strolling along the boardwalks while watching the birds fly gracefully above the water. The reflections of the mountains on the lake create a picturesque setting, and the chance to see wildlife makes it even more special.

For those interested in spotting wolves, the best chance is around the hay fields near the town of Banff and along the Icefields Parkway. Wolves are generally more active during dawn and dusk, so early mornings or late evenings are the best times to look for them. It can be a bit challenging to spot them, but the thrill of possibly seeing a wolf pack in action is worth the wait.

As you explore these areas, remember to practice safe wildlife viewing. Stay in your vehicle when possible, keep a safe distance from animals, and never approach them. This helps keep both you and the wildlife safe. Bring binoculars for a better view, and a camera to capture the memories of these incredible creatures in their natural surroundings.

Banff National Park offers numerous fantastic wildlife viewing areas like the Bow Valley Parkway, Lake Minnewanka, Johnston Canyon, and Vermilion Lakes. Each location provides unique opportunities to connect with nature and witness the beauty of wildlife. Whether you're driving, hiking, or simply enjoying the view, you'll find that the park's rich wildlife adds to the magic of your experience.

How to Safely View Wildlife

Seeing wildlife in Banff National Park can be one of the most exciting parts of your visit, but it's important to do it safely and responsibly. Understanding how to view animals without disturbing them helps protect both the wildlife and yourself.

First, always keep a safe distance from animals. This means staying at least 100 yards away from bears and wolves and 25 yards away from elk and deer. Animals can be unpredictable, especially if they feel threatened or cornered. Using binoculars or a camera with a zoom lens allows you to see them up close without getting too close. I remember watching a mother elk and her calf from a distance while enjoying the tranquility of the surroundings.

When you're driving through the park, be sure to pull over safely if you spot wildlife. Look for designated pull-outs where you can park your car. This keeps the road clear for other vehicles and makes it safer for you to observe the animals. Avoid stopping in the middle of the road, as it can cause accidents and annoy other drivers.

It's also important to remain quiet. Loud noises can scare animals away or cause them to act defensively. Speaking softly and keeping movements slow helps to keep wildlife calm. I once watched a herd of deer feeding in a meadow, and the stillness of the moment made it feel like I was part of their world.

Avoid feeding wildlife, as it can lead to dangerous situations for both you and the animals. Feeding them changes their natural behavior and can make them reliant on humans for food. This can lead to aggressive encounters, especially if they feel threatened or if someone gets too close.

If you encounter a bear, stay calm and back away slowly. Never run, as this may trigger a chase instinct. Make your presence known by talking in a calm voice and waving your arms to appear larger. It's important to know what to do if you see a bear. Most of the time, they will move on if they see you.

In addition to being cautious around wildlife, it's wise to be aware of your surroundings. Always check the trail signs and park guidelines for any specific wildlife warnings. If you're hiking, travel in groups if possible, as this can help deter wildlife encounters.

Always carry bear spray when hiking in bear country. It's a precautionary measure that can help protect you in case of an unexpected encounter. Make sure you know how to use it properly before you go out on the trails.

Respecting wildlife means observing from a distance and not trying to provoke them. Avoid loud noises, sudden movements, or any behavior that may disturb them.

Safely viewing wildlife in Banff National Park requires patience, respect, and awareness. By keeping a safe distance, remaining quiet, and being cautious in your actions, you can have an enjoyable experience while protecting the amazing creatures that call the park home. Every wildlife sighting can be magical, and with a little care, you can create lasting memories while ensuring their safety and yours.

Understanding the Park's Conservation Efforts

Banff National Park is not just a beautiful place to visit; it's also a vital area for conservation. Understanding the park's efforts to protect its natural environment and wildlife helps visitors appreciate the area even more.

One of the main goals of conservation in Banff is to maintain the delicate balance of the ecosystem. The park is home to a variety of animals and plants, each playing a crucial role in the environment. By protecting these species, the park ensures that everything from the smallest flower to the largest grizzly bear can thrive. I often find it fascinating to learn how interconnected everything is, from the rivers that flow through the valleys to the forests that blanket the mountains.

To support wildlife, the park has created wildlife corridors. These are safe pathways that animals can use to travel between different areas without being disrupted by human activity or roads. For instance, bears often need to move over large distances in search of food or mates, and these corridors help them do that safely. I once stood at a viewing point and was lucky enough to see a bear using one of these paths, which reminded me of the importance of keeping natural routes open.

Banff also focuses on protecting its waters. Clean water is essential for all living things, and the park actively monitors rivers and lakes to keep them healthy. They work on restoring areas that have been damaged and ensuring that pollution from nearby roads and developments is kept to a minimum. When I paddle in the crystal-clear waters of Lake Louise, I'm reminded of how vital these efforts are to maintain such beauty.

Another important aspect of conservation is managing visitors. With millions of people coming to the park each year, it's essential to have rules in place to protect the environment. There are designated trails for hiking and biking, which help reduce the impact on the surrounding nature. Staying on these trails not only protects fragile habitats but also makes for a safer experience. I've found that following these paths often leads to the most breathtaking views and hidden gems.

Education plays a huge role in the park's conservation efforts. Park rangers and guides provide information on local wildlife, plants, and the importance of conservation. They help visitors understand why it's crucial to respect nature and how even small actions can make a difference. During a guided tour, I learned about the park's history and the challenges it faces, which deepened my appreciation for the land.

Banff National Park is also involved in research. Scientists study the effects of climate change on the park's ecosystems, looking at how warming temperatures and shifting weather patterns impact wildlife. This research is vital for developing strategies to protect the park in the future. I remember seeing researchers working in the field, collecting data that will help inform future conservation efforts.

Another exciting initiative is the park's commitment to restoring habitats. When areas have been damaged by development or natural disasters, the park works to rehabilitate them. This might include planting native species or creating barriers to prevent erosion. I've seen areas that have been restored, and it's inspiring to witness nature bouncing back over time.

Supporting local communities is part of Banff's conservation efforts. The park collaborates with nearby towns to promote sustainable tourism. This means encouraging visitors to respect local cultures and use resources wisely. I often enjoy local events and markets, knowing that my participation helps support the community and its conservation initiatives.

Understanding Banff National Park's conservation efforts enriches the experience of visiting this stunning area. By knowing how the park protects its wildlife, waters, and ecosystems, visitors can play a part in these efforts. Whether it's staying on trails, participating in educational programs, or simply appreciating the beauty around them, everyone can contribute to keeping Banff a vibrant and healthy environment for future generations.

CHAPTER EIGHT

DAY TRIP AND EXCURSIONS

Icefields Parkway: A Scenic Drive to Jasper

Driving along the Icefields Parkway is like entering a postcard. This famous route stretches for about 230 kilometers (143 miles) between Banff and Jasper and is one of the most beautiful drives in the world. As I set out on this journey, I felt a thrill of excitement knowing that stunning views awaited me at every turn.

The adventure begins in Banff National Park. The road is well-maintained and easy to navigate. Right from the start, I was greeted by towering mountains, lush forests, and sparkling lakes. It was like nature was putting on a show just for me. I found myself stopping frequently to take photos and soak in the views.

One of the first highlights along the Icefields Parkway is Lake Louise. Even though I had visited before, seeing it from this angle was a different experience. The lake's vibrant turquoise water, surrounded by snow-capped peaks, was just as breathtaking as ever. I recommend taking a few minutes to stretch your legs here and enjoy the scenery.

Continuing on, I approached the Bow Lake viewpoint. This is a perfect spot to stop and enjoy the view of Bow Lake and the impressive Bow Glacier in the background. I parked my car and walked a short distance to the viewpoint. The sight of the glacier cascading down the mountain was awe-inspiring.

There's a peaceful atmosphere here, and it's a great place to relax for a moment.

As I drove further, I reached the Columbia Icefield. This massive icefield is one of the largest in North America and is home to the famous Athabasca Glacier. There are various tours available, including guided walks onto the glacier itself. I chose to take a short tour, which was an unforgettable experience. Standing on the ancient ice and learning about its formation gave me a deeper appreciation for this natural wonder. If you're up for it, don't miss the chance to step onto the glacier.

Along the Icefields Parkway, wildlife sightings are common. I was lucky enough to spot some elk grazing by the roadside, and I even saw a black bear in the distance. Remember to drive slowly and be cautious, as wildlife can appear unexpectedly. It's important to respect their space and not get too close.

As I continued my journey, the scenery kept changing. The mountains became even more dramatic, with jagged peaks reaching for the sky. The deep blue of the lakes contrasted beautifully with the green of the forests. Every few kilometers, there's a lookout point where I could stop and take in the breathtaking views. I recommend bringing binoculars if you want to spot more wildlife or enjoy the scenery from a distance.

The journey culminates as I arrive in Jasper National Park. The town of Jasper has a charming atmosphere, with cozy cafes and shops. After a long day of driving, it felt great to unwind in this welcoming town. I enjoyed a delicious meal at one of the local restaurants, where I could reflect on the stunning sights I had witnessed along the Icefields Parkway.

For anyone planning this drive, I suggest starting early in the day to make the most of the light and to avoid crowds. Bringing snacks and drinks can make the trip more enjoyable, especially since there are several scenic picnic spots along the way. It's also wise to check the weather before heading out, as conditions can change quickly in the mountains.

The Icefields Parkway is more than just a road; it's a journey through some of the most beautiful landscapes in Canada. Whether you're an avid photographer, a nature lover, or just looking for a peaceful drive, this route has something for everyone. From sparkling lakes to towering glaciers and abundant wildlife, the memories made on this drive will last a lifetime. So grab your camera, hit the road, and get ready for an unforgettable adventure.

Yoho National Park: Emerald Lake and Takakkaw Falls

Visiting Yoho National Park is like stepping into a world of stunning natural beauty. One of the park's highlights is Emerald Lake, a true gem surrounded by towering mountains. When I first caught sight of the lake, its vibrant turquoise color took my breath away. The water is so clear that you can see reflections of the surrounding peaks, creating a magical atmosphere.

To get to Emerald Lake, I drove from the nearby town of Field, which is just a short distance away. The drive itself is scenic, with beautiful views of the landscape. Upon arriving, I parked at the visitor center and took a short walk to the lake. The path is well-marked, making it easy to navigate. As I approached the lake, I was greeted by the soothing sounds of water lapping against the shore.

Walking along the shoreline is a must. There are several viewpoints where I stopped to take photos and soak in the beauty. The peaceful setting made it a perfect place to relax and unwind. I found a lovely spot to sit on a bench and enjoy a picnic while taking in the views. I recommend bringing snacks and a drink to make the most of your time here.

If you're feeling adventurous, you can rent a canoe and paddle on the lake. Gliding across the water gives a unique perspective of the surrounding mountains. The tranquility of being on the lake is something I cherished. Watching the sun dance on the surface of the water was mesmerizing.

After spending time at Emerald Lake, I decided to visit Takakkaw Falls, another highlight of Yoho National Park. The falls are located about 15 minutes away by car. The drive is scenic, with winding roads that lead you deeper into the heart of the park. Upon arriving, I parked in the designated area and walked a short trail to the falls.

When I reached the viewpoint, the sight was incredible. Takakkaw Falls is one of Canada's highest waterfalls, plunging 254 meters (833 feet) down the rocky cliffs. The roar of the water was powerful, and mist filled the air, creating a refreshing atmosphere. I felt a sense of awe standing in front of such a magnificent sight.

The trail around the falls offers several viewpoints, each providing a different angle of the cascading water. I took my time exploring, snapping photos, and enjoying the surroundings. There's something truly special about being so close to nature's power.

If you're visiting in summer, the falls are particularly impressive as the snow melts, creating a strong flow of water. There are also picnic areas nearby where you can enjoy a meal while listening to the sound of the falls in the background. It's a great way to relax and take in the scenery.

For those traveling on a budget, both Emerald Lake and Takakkaw Falls offer free access. Just be sure to bring your own food and drinks to save money. The park is also a great place for hiking. There are numerous trails in the area that cater to different skill levels, allowing everyone to explore and enjoy the park's beauty.

Yoho National Park, with its breathtaking Emerald Lake and impressive Takakkaw Falls, is a must-visit destination for nature lovers. Whether you're looking to relax by the lake, paddle in a canoe, or feel the mist from a waterfall, there's something for everyone. This park is a true showcase of Canada's natural beauty, and I recommend setting aside a day to experience its wonders. Grab your camera, pack a picnic, and get ready for an unforgettable adventure in Yoho National Park.

Kootenay National Park: Radium Hot Springs and Paint Pots

Kootenay National Park is a beautiful place to explore, with unique attractions like Radium Hot Springs and the Paint Pots. Each offers a different kind of adventure and stunning views of nature.

Starting with Radium Hot Springs, this spot is famous for its relaxing thermal waters. When I arrived, I could already feel the warm air coming from the springs. The hot springs are located just a few minutes from the town of Radium Hot Springs, which is easy to find along Highway 93/95. There's plenty of parking available, making it convenient to access.

The springs are part of a larger pool area that includes a family-friendly pool and a more tranquil one for adults. As I stepped into the hot springs, the warm water felt amazing against my skin. It was such a nice contrast to the cool mountain air. The views from the pool are incredible, with the surrounding mountains creating a stunning backdrop. I spent a good amount of time relaxing in the water, soaking in the peaceful atmosphere. There are also areas to lounge and enjoy snacks, making it a perfect spot for a day trip.

After enjoying the hot springs, I decided to visit the Paint Pots, which are about a 30-minute drive from Radium Hot Springs. The Paint Pots are a fascinating natural phenomenon featuring colorful mud pools created by iron oxide. To get there, I drove along Kootenay Park Highway, enjoying the scenic views of the mountains and forests along the way. There's a designated parking area, and the trailhead is clearly marked.

The hike to the Paint Pots is short and relatively easy, making it suitable for families and casual walkers. As I walked along the trail, I could feel the excitement building. The path winds through beautiful scenery, and the sound of birds and rustling leaves adds to the experience.

When I finally reached the Paint Pots, I was mesmerized. The vibrant colors of the mud pools, ranging from bright orange to deep red, were striking against the green of the surrounding forest. The sight felt almost surreal. There are wooden boardwalks that let you get a closer look at the pools without disturbing them. I spent time admiring the colors and taking photos.

What makes the Paint Pots special is the natural bubbling action that occurs when water mixes with the clay. It's like watching nature at work, and I found it quite fascinating.

After exploring the Paint Pots, I took the time to relax in the nearby picnic area. There are benches and tables where visitors can enjoy a meal while surrounded by nature. I recommend packing a lunch to enjoy here, as it's a perfect spot to take in the scenery.

For travelers on a budget, both Radium Hot Springs and the Paint Pots offer affordable options for a day of fun. The hot springs have an entry fee, but it's well worth it for the experience. The Paint Pots, on the other hand, are free to visit, allowing you to explore without spending much.

Kootenay National Park is a wonderful destination filled with natural wonders. Radium Hot Springs is perfect for relaxation, while the Paint Pots offer a unique and colorful experience. Whether you're soaking in the hot springs or marveling at the vibrant mud pools, you'll find something to love in this beautiful park. Don't forget to bring your camera and pack some snacks to make the most of your visit!

Exploring Canmore and the Bow Valley

Exploring Canmore and the Bow Valley is like stepping into a picture-perfect postcard. Nestled between the stunning Rocky Mountains, Canmore is a charming town with a friendly vibe that draws visitors from all over. Getting there is easy; just take the Trans-Canada Highway (Highway 1) from Calgary, and in about an hour, you'll be surrounded by beautiful mountain scenery.

Once you arrive in Canmore, the first thing that strikes you is the breathtaking views. The majestic mountains tower over the town, creating a stunning backdrop for your adventure. One of the best ways to take it all in is by strolling along the Canmore Nordic Centre, located at 1988 Olympic Way. The centre is perfect for hiking, biking, and even cross-country skiing in winter. I enjoyed biking along the well-maintained trails, which offered stunning views of the Bow Valley.

After some outdoor activity, I explored Canmore's Main Street. This area is full of unique shops, cozy cafes, and local restaurants. One of my favorite spots is the Canmore Brewing Company at 101, 1040 Railway Ave, where you can sample delicious craft beers made right in town. The atmosphere is relaxed, and it's a great place to chat with locals and fellow travelers.

For a taste of local cuisine, I highly recommend The Bison Restaurant & Terrace at 202 Bowness Ave. The menu features fresh, locally sourced ingredients, and the ambiance is welcoming. I tried their bison burger, which was juicy and flavorful, paired with some crispy fries.

If you're in the mood for something sweet, don't miss the Rocky Mountain Chocolate Factory at 1200 Railway Ave. Their handmade chocolates and treats are heavenly. I couldn't resist picking up a few chocolate-covered strawberries to enjoy later.

Another must-see in the Bow Valley is the Bow Valley Wildland Provincial Park. This area is perfect for hiking and wildlife spotting. You can find various trails that suit all levels of hikers. I hiked the Grassi Lakes Trail, starting from the parking lot at 250, 300 Grassi Lakes Rd. The trail is moderately challenging but offers incredible views of turquoise lakes and surrounding mountains. The vibrant colors of the lakes are stunning and worth every step of the hike.

If you're looking for something more relaxing, consider heading to the Canmore River for a leisurely walk along the Bow River Pathway. The pathway is easy to follow and offers beautiful views of the river, with opportunities to spot wildlife along the way. I saw ducks swimming and even spotted a few deer grazing nearby.

As the day winds down, you can unwind by visiting one of Canmore's spas or wellness centers. Many places offer massages and treatments that are perfect for relaxing after a day of adventure. I found a lovely little spa called Serenity Spa, where I enjoyed a soothing massage that helped me recharge.

For those planning a longer stay, there are various accommodations available in Canmore, from cozy inns to vacation rentals. Staying in Canmore is a great base for exploring the Bow Valley and nearby attractions like Banff National Park, just a short drive away.

Exploring Canmore and the Bow Valley offers a delightful mix of outdoor adventures, local culture, and stunning landscapes. Whether you're hiking in the mountains, enjoying local food, or simply taking in the breathtaking views, Canmore is a destination that will leave you with lasting memories. Don't forget your camera; the scenery is too beautiful to miss!

CHAPTER NINE

LOCAL FOOD AND DINING EXPERIENCE

Top Restaurants and Cafés in Banff

When it comes to dining and nightlife in Banff National Park, visitors are spoiled with a range of options that reflect the park's unique charm, natural bounty, and cultural influences. Whether you're in the mood for a high-end meal, a cozy bite, or something in between, Banff offers dining experiences that suit every taste and budget. Below is a comprehensive guide to some must-try local eateries, each offering something distinct and memorable for visitors.

The dining scene in Banff National Park celebrates the area's pristine environment, with many restaurants focusing on local ingredients and sustainable practices. From farm-to-table eateries to hidden gems nestled away from the main drag, these spots offer an opportunity to savor regional cuisine with a Rocky Mountain twist.

1. The Bison Restaurant & Terrace
Location: 211 Bear St, Banff, AB T1L 1E4
Atmosphere: The Bison is an upscale yet relaxed dining venue, with large windows that allow natural light to pour in, giving you a perfect view of the surrounding mountains. The vibe is both romantic and welcoming, making it ideal for couples, families, or a special celebration.
Pricing: Moderate to high-end. Expect appetizers to range between $15 to $25, while main courses cost between $35 and $50. Desserts hover around $12 to $15.

Signature Dishes: The restaurant highlights local ingredients like Alberta beef, wild game, and sustainably sourced fish. Their bison short ribs are a must-try, slow-cooked and tender, paired with seasonal vegetables. Another popular dish is the wild boar and bison burger, which perfectly blends flavors with house-made condiments.

2. The Maple Leaf Grill & Lounge
Location: 137 Banff Ave, Banff, AB T1L 1C8
Atmosphere: This cozy yet elegant restaurant is quintessentially Canadian, both in its decor and menu. Featuring warm wood interiors, the ambiance is rustic with a touch of sophistication. It's a great spot for a romantic dinner or a special occasion with friends.
Pricing: Mid to high-end. Appetizers typically range from $12 to $20, mains from $30 to $50, and desserts around $10 to $14.
Signature Dishes: Known for its locally sourced ingredients, The Maple Leaf offers standout dishes like their Alberta beef tenderloin and cedar plank salmon. Their use of Canadian ingredients like maple glaze and seasonal root vegetables elevates these classics to a whole new level. The seafood platter is another favorite, offering a taste of fresh oysters, lobster, and salmon.

3. Tooloulou's
Location: 204 Caribou St, Banff, AB T1L 1C3
Atmosphere: Tooloulou's is a casual, family-friendly spot with a Creole-inspired twist. The decor is vibrant and eclectic, offering a fun, laid-back atmosphere. It's perfect for a quick

bite, a hearty breakfast, or a relaxed dinner with friends or family.

Pricing: Affordable to moderate. Most appetizers are around $8 to $15, with main courses ranging from $18 to $25. Breakfast dishes are particularly popular and are very reasonably priced, averaging around $10 to $15.

Signature Dishes: Tooloulou's is known for its Cajun-style dishes with a Canadian touch. Try their classic jambalaya, packed with shrimp, sausage, and chicken. For breakfast lovers, their French toast made with fresh berries is a crowd favorite. The portions are generous, so you'll definitely leave satisfied.

4. Park Distillery Restaurant and Bar

Location: 219 Banff Ave, Banff, AB T1L 1B2

Atmosphere: Park Distillery offers a campfire-inspired atmosphere, with the vibe of a rustic mountain lodge. It's casual and relaxed, making it a great place to hang out after a day of hiking or skiing. With its in-house distillery, the restaurant also has a lively bar scene.

Pricing: Moderate. Appetizers cost between $12 and $18, mains from $25 to $40, and cocktails are priced at around $12 to $15.

Signature Dishes: The campfire chicken is a must-try, cooked over an open flame, bringing out a rich, smoky flavor. Their smoked brisket sandwich and the grilled rainbow trout are also popular choices. Be sure to try their house-made spirits, especially in one of their signature cocktails, like the Park Sour.

5. Eden at The Rimrock Resort

Location: 300 Mountain Ave, Banff, AB T1L 1J2

Atmosphere: Eden is a high-end, fine-dining experience that is perfect for special occasions. The ambiance is elegant, and the dining room boasts panoramic views of the Rockies. With impeccable service and attention to detail, it offers an intimate and sophisticated atmosphere.

Pricing: High-end. Appetizers are priced around $20 to $35, while main courses start at $50 and can go as high as $90 depending on the dish. Desserts are typically $15 to $20.

Signature Dishes: Eden specializes in French-inspired cuisine using local ingredients. Their multi-course tasting menu is the highlight, featuring dishes like seared foie gras, Alberta lamb, and wild mushroom risotto. For dessert, their artisanal chocolate creations are a sweet end to the meal.

6. Three Ravens Restaurant & Wine Bar

Location: 107 Tunnel Mountain Dr, Banff, AB T1L 1H5

Atmosphere: Located at the Banff Centre for Arts and Creativity, Three Ravens offers a modern, upscale setting with floor-to-ceiling windows that provide an incredible view of the Bow Valley. The atmosphere is sophisticated yet welcoming, with a focus on creative culinary presentations.

Pricing: High-end. Appetizers cost around $15 to $25, and mains range from $40 to $60. A full-course meal, including wine, can run from $100 to $150 per person.

Signature Dishes: The menu changes seasonally, but their wild game offerings, like elk and venison, are always a highlight. The chef's attention to detail shines through in every dish, particularly in their house-made pastas and intricate desserts like the chocolate mousse with hazelnut praline.

Nightlife in Banff

Though it's known for its daytime adventures, Banff has a lively nightlife scene that keeps things interesting after the sun sets. Most of the nightlife in Banff is centered around Banff Avenue, where you'll find pubs, lounges, and clubs buzzing with energy.

For a casual night out, Rose & Crown Pub at 202 Banff Ave is a popular spot. The vibe is lively, with live music often playing in the background. The rooftop patio is a great place to enjoy a drink with mountain views. If you're in the mood for something a little more upscale, head to High Rollers at 110 Banff Ave, where you can enjoy craft beer, bowling, and even a pizza menu while soaking in the laid-back atmosphere.

For something a little more refined, The Bear Street Tavern at 211 Bear St serves up a relaxed environment, where you can enjoy specialty cocktails and wood-fired pizzas in a cozy setting.

Whether you're looking for an adventurous night out or a quiet evening sipping local brews, Banff has something to offer for everyone.

Farm-to-Table Dining and Local Ingredients

Farm-to-table dining in Banff is a wonderful way to experience the region's natural bounty and culinary creativity. With its emphasis on fresh, locally sourced ingredients, this style of dining celebrates the flavors of the surrounding landscapes. Banff's restaurants take pride in offering dishes that highlight the best of what the area has to offer, from wild game and freshwater fish to farm-grown vegetables and organic produce.

Many of Banff's farm-to-table restaurants focus on sustainability, partnering with local farmers, ranchers, and fishermen to ensure that their ingredients are not only fresh but also ethically sourced. This commitment to the environment and the local economy gives diners the opportunity to enjoy meals that are both delicious and rooted in the region's agricultural traditions.

One of the standout spots for farm-to-table dining is The Bison Restaurant. This place is known for its focus on regional ingredients, with a menu that features locally raised meats, fresh produce, and house-made condiments. Their bison dishes, in particular, are a testament to the restaurant's dedication to showcasing Alberta's finest meats. Whether it's their slow-cooked bison short ribs or the wild boar and bison burger, you'll experience rich, hearty flavors that are truly local. Vegetables are often sourced from nearby farms, ensuring that the freshness shines through in every bite.

Another excellent farm-to-table experience is found at The Maple Leaf Grill, which celebrates Canadian ingredients like Alberta beef, Pacific seafood, and seasonal vegetables. Their cedar plank salmon is a popular choice, featuring locally caught fish paired with farm-fresh sides like roasted root vegetables. The care they take in selecting ingredients means that the flavors are always bold and vibrant, reflecting the best of Canadian cuisine.

For a more casual farm-to-table experience, Wild Flour Bakery is a great option. This cozy spot focuses on organic, locally sourced ingredients to create fresh breads, pastries, and sandwiches. The emphasis here is on quality, with simple yet flavorful combinations that highlight the natural goodness of the ingredients. Whether you're stopping in for a quick breakfast or a light lunch, Wild Flour Bakery offers an authentic taste of Banff's food scene.

In addition to restaurants, local farmers' markets are also a great way to get a sense of the farm-to-table culture in Banff. These markets often feature fresh produce, meats, cheeses, and baked goods from nearby farms, giving visitors the opportunity to sample local ingredients and take home a piece of Banff's culinary heritage.

What sets farm-to-table dining apart is the direct connection between the food on your plate and the land around you. By dining at these establishments, you're not only supporting local farmers and producers but also enjoying meals that are full of fresh, vibrant flavors. The chefs in Banff take great care in crafting dishes that tell a story about the region's rich agricultural roots, offering diners a truly immersive experience.

Whether you're dining at an upscale restaurant or grabbing a bite at a local café, Banff's farm-to-table offerings give you a taste of the Rockies in every dish. From the freshness of the vegetables to the quality of the meats, the ingredients speak for themselves, making each meal a memorable part of your visit to Banff National Park.

Craft Breweries and Local Beverages

Banff's craft breweries and local beverages scene offers a fantastic way to explore the unique flavors of the Rockies. Whether you're looking to unwind after a day of outdoor adventure or simply want to sample some regional drinks, the town has a growing collection of breweries and bars that highlight local ingredients and creative brewing techniques.

The most popular craft brewery in Banff is Banff Ave Brewing Co., located right in the heart of town. The atmosphere here is casual and welcoming, with big windows that offer great views of the surrounding mountains while you sip on a cold beer. The brewery's lineup includes a variety of handcrafted beers, many of which are inspired by the local environment. One of their must-try beers is the Head Smashed IPA, which is bold, hoppy, and full of character. If you're into lighter beers, their Lower Bankhead Lager is a refreshing option that's perfect for a warm day after a hike. The food menu also pairs nicely with the drinks, offering everything from burgers to shareable snacks.

Another great place for local brews is Three Bears Brewery & Restaurant. This brewery blends the outdoor spirit of Banff with cozy, modern interiors. The beer is brewed on-site, and you can actually see the brewing equipment from some of the seating areas. Their signature Three Bears Pale Ale is smooth, with a balanced flavor that makes it easy to enjoy. For those who like trying something different, the Grizzly Bear

Blueberry Ale is a fun choice, with subtle fruit notes that don't overwhelm the taste of the beer. It's a great spot to relax, enjoy a meal, and taste some of the Rockies in every glass.

If you're more into spirits, Park Distillery is a must-visit. Located along Banff Avenue, this distillery is all about using pure mountain water and natural ingredients to create high-quality, small-batch spirits. They produce everything from vodka and gin to whiskey, all crafted with a focus on local and sustainable ingredients. Their Glacier Rye is a favorite among whiskey lovers, with a smooth, slightly spicy finish. The vodka, made from 100% Alberta grains, is also exceptional, and you can enjoy it neat or in one of their creative cocktails. The distillery also has a restaurant that serves up delicious, mountain-inspired dishes.

For wine lovers, while Banff doesn't have vineyards of its own, many restaurants and bars carry excellent Canadian wines from nearby regions like the Okanagan Valley in British Columbia. This area is known for producing fantastic wines, and many local spots in Banff pride themselves on offering an extensive selection of reds, whites, and rosés to pair with your meal.

When it comes to beverages in Banff, it's not just about alcohol. Many cafes and coffee shops in town also serve locally roasted coffee and teas. Wild Flour Bakery, for example, serves a variety of locally sourced drinks that go perfectly with their fresh pastries and sandwiches.

What makes Banff's craft beer and beverage scene special is the connection to the local landscape. Whether it's the pure glacier water used in spirits or the mountain-inspired flavors of the beers, each drink gives you a taste of the Rockies. The relaxed, welcoming atmosphere of these spots makes them the perfect place to wind down, meet fellow travelers, and enjoy the local flavors.

If you're exploring Banff, be sure to stop by one of these craft breweries or distilleries, try a locally made drink, and soak in the beautiful surroundings. Each sip will remind you of the natural beauty and unique charm of the area.

CHAPTER TEN
ADVENTUROUS ACTIVITIES BEYOND
THE TRAILS

Rock Climbing and Via Ferrata Routes

Rock climbing and Via Ferrata routes in Banff offer an exciting way to experience the towering peaks and rugged beauty of the Canadian Rockies. Whether you're a seasoned climber or trying these activities for the first time, the stunning views and thrilling routes make it a memorable adventure.

One of the most accessible places for rock climbing is the Cascade Mountain area, which is close to Banff town. Cascade Mountain offers a variety of climbing routes for different skill levels. To get here, drive along the Trans-Canada Highway, and you'll find a parking lot at the Cascade Ponds. From here, it's a short hike to the base of the mountain where the climbing begins. The routes vary in difficulty, but beginners might want to start with easier climbs like Cascade Falls, which is not too technical but still offers a thrilling challenge. The rock quality is generally good, and the views over Banff are breathtaking. Make sure to bring the necessary climbing gear or book with a local guide if you're not experienced in lead climbing.

If you're looking for a more guided and secure climbing experience, Via Ferrata at Mount Norquay is a fantastic option. This guided climbing route allows you to scale mountain cliffs with the safety of fixed cables and iron rungs.

It's designed for those who may not have much rock climbing experience but still want to feel the exhilaration of climbing steep mountainsides. Located just a short drive from Banff, Mount Norquay is easily accessible, and the Via Ferrata experience can be booked directly through their website or at the base of the mountain. There are several routes to choose from, ranging from a two-hour beginner's course to a six-hour full-day adventure. On my trip, I tried the Ridgewalker route, which takes around four hours and leads to spectacular ridge views. The best part is that you're always safely clipped into the system, so even those with a fear of heights can enjoy the climb. The guide was friendly and made sure everyone felt comfortable and safe.

For those wanting to test their climbing skills a bit further, Lake Louise has some excellent rock climbing routes as well. The Quartzite Crag near the Lake Louise Ski Resort is a popular climbing area. You can park at the base of the ski resort and hike about 20 minutes to reach the climbing site. This spot has a variety of sport climbing routes that range in difficulty, making it suitable for both beginners and advanced climbers. The quartzite rock is great for climbing and provides solid holds as you ascend. The views of Lake Louise and the surrounding glaciers are simply incredible, making the effort well worth it. I loved the sense of peace and isolation while climbing here, away from the busier tourist areas.

If you're new to climbing or Via Ferrata, Banff has several guiding companies that offer tours and training. Yamnuska Mountain Adventures is one of the well-known guide companies in the region, and they offer everything from beginner climbing lessons to more advanced alpine climbing trips. It's always a good idea to climb with a guide if you're not familiar with the area or the techniques, as they can ensure safety and provide all the gear you need.

Rock climbing and Via Ferrata in Banff are great ways to experience the dramatic landscapes up close. Whether you're scaling the side of a mountain or carefully navigating a Via Ferrata route, you'll be rewarded with stunning views and a real sense of accomplishment. The thrill of reaching the top and looking out over the endless mountain ranges is something you'll never forget.

If you're planning to try rock climbing or Via Ferrata in Banff, make sure to check the weather beforehand, dress in layers, and always bring enough water. Even in the summer, temperatures can drop at higher altitudes, and it's important to stay comfortable while climbing. If you're ready for a challenge and some of the best mountain views, this is an experience you won't want to miss!

Mountain Biking Trails

Mountain biking in Banff is an exhilarating way to explore the stunning landscapes of the Canadian Rockies. The area offers a variety of trails for all skill levels, from easy forest paths to more challenging mountain routes, each offering breathtaking views and a sense of adventure.

One of the most popular trails for beginners is the Tunnel Mountain Trail. It's close to Banff town, making it easy to access. You can start at the Tunnel Mountain Campground (302 Tunnel Mountain Rd, Banff, AB T1L 1B3). From here, the trail winds through gentle terrain, offering beautiful views of the town and surrounding mountains. The ride is relatively easy, making it perfect for families or those new to mountain biking. The forested path provides shade, and the peaceful environment makes it a relaxing ride. I remember my first time biking here—the feeling of riding under the towering pines and the views of Cascade Mountain made it a memorable experience without being too strenuous.

For a slightly more challenging ride, the Spray River Loop is a fantastic option. This trail takes you along the Spray River, offering stunning views of the water and surrounding mountains. The trailhead is located near the Banff Springs Hotel (405 Spray Ave, Banff, AB T1L 1J4). The loop is about 12 kilometers long and mostly flat, but there are a few moderate climbs along the way. The path is wide and well-maintained, making it suitable for intermediate riders. I enjoyed the mix of forest and open views, and the trail crosses two bridges, giving you different perspectives of the river. It's a peaceful ride, with few crowds, especially in the early mornings.

For more advanced mountain bikers, the Lake Minnewanka Shoreline Trail offers a thrilling ride. You can start from the Lake Minnewanka parking lot (Lake Minnewanka Scenic Dr, Banff, AB T0L 2C0), and the trail hugs the shoreline of the lake, providing stunning water views throughout the ride. This trail is longer and more technical, with rocky sections and some steep climbs. It's about 30 kilometers round trip if you go all the way to the end of the trail, but you can turn around at any point if you prefer a shorter ride. The scenery here is absolutely spectacular, with the turquoise waters of Lake Minnewanka on one side and towering cliffs on the other. On my last trip, I took several breaks just to sit by the water and soak in the views.

For those looking for a real challenge, the Highline Trail near Canmore is a demanding but rewarding ride. Canmore is just a short drive from Banff, and the trailhead can be accessed from Three Sisters Parkway (10 minutes from Canmore town center). The Highline Trail is steep and rocky, with technical sections that require good bike handling skills. The views, though, are some of the best in the area, with sweeping panoramas of the Bow Valley and surrounding peaks. This is a trail for experienced bikers who want to push themselves and enjoy an adventure off the beaten path. I remember the sense of achievement I felt after completing this trail—it's tough, but the views and the ride down make it all worth it.

If you don't have your own bike, there are plenty of places in Banff where you can rent mountain bikes. Soul Ski & Bike (203 Bear St, Banff, AB T1L 1H4) is a popular option, offering rentals for all skill levels. The staff are knowledgeable and can recommend trails based on your experience. There are also guided mountain biking tours available if you're unfamiliar with the area and prefer to have a guide show you the best trails.

Mountain biking in Banff is not only about the thrill of the ride but also about being surrounded by nature. Whether you're riding through a peaceful forest or along the edge of a sparkling lake, the experience is unforgettable. Just be sure to bring plenty of water, wear appropriate safety gear, and check the weather before heading out. The trails can be unpredictable, and it's always a good idea to be prepared. With so many trails to choose from, mountain biking in Banff offers something for everyone, from casual riders to experienced bikers looking for a challenge. It's a great way to explore the national park and see the stunning Rocky Mountains from a different perspective.

Horseback Riding Adventures

Horseback riding in Banff National Park is a unique way to experience the natural beauty of the Rockies. There's something magical about seeing towering mountains, thick forests, and crystal-clear rivers from the back of a horse, just as explorers once did. Whether you're an experienced rider or trying it for the first time, Banff offers a variety of horseback riding adventures that allow you to connect with nature in a slower, more peaceful way.

One of the best places to start is with Banff Trail Riders, a well-known horseback riding outfitter in the area. They are located at 100 Sundance Rd, Banff, AB T1L 1B9, just a short walk from the Banff town center. Banff Trail Riders offers several options, from short rides to full-day adventures, so you can choose based on your comfort level and how much time you have.

For beginners or those short on time, the Bow River Ride is perfect. It's a one-hour ride along the scenic Bow River, where you'll enjoy stunning views of Cascade Mountain and the surrounding wilderness. The gentle pace of the horses makes it a relaxing experience, and the guides are friendly, sharing stories about the area's history and wildlife. I remember feeling completely at ease as the horses calmly navigated the trail, allowing me to fully take in the beauty of the river and the forests around us.

If you're up for a longer ride, the Sundance Loop Ride is a great choice. This ride takes about 2-3 hours and leads you through more rugged terrain, including open meadows, dense forests, and higher viewpoints that offer incredible panoramas of the surrounding peaks. The trail is well-maintained, and the horses are experienced, making it suitable even for those with little riding experience. The highlight for me was reaching a spot overlooking the Bow Valley, where we paused to take in the vastness of the landscape. It felt like stepping back in time, with no sounds but the rustle of trees and the occasional call of a bird.

For those looking for an all-day adventure, the Sundance Lodge Overnight Trip is an unforgettable experience. You'll spend the day riding deeper into the wilderness, passing rivers, mountains, and remote areas few people get to see. After a day on horseback, you'll arrive at Sundance Lodge, a cozy backcountry lodge where you can relax, enjoy a hearty meal, and sleep in comfort. Waking up to the quiet of the wilderness, with no cell phone signal and nothing but nature around you, is an experience I'll never forget. It's a great way to truly escape the modern world and reconnect with the natural environment.

Another option for horseback riding is at Cross Zee Ranch, located just outside Banff at 12 Cross Zee Rd, Canmore, AB T1W 2X2. This ranch offers shorter rides perfect for families, with calm horses and easy trails that allow even the youngest riders to enjoy the experience. The staff at Cross Zee Ranch are incredibly welcoming and take great care to match riders with the right horse based on their comfort and experience level. I visited with a group of friends who had never ridden before, and everyone felt confident and excited after the ride.

We loved how peaceful it felt to trot through the fields, surrounded by mountains on all sides.

For a more adventurous ride, you can head out to Lake Louise, where horseback rides will take you up into the alpine. Timberline Tours, located at Lake Louise Dr, Lake Louise, AB T0L 1E0, offers a variety of rides, including a popular trail to the Lake Agnes Tea House. The ride up is both challenging and rewarding, with the horses skillfully navigating rocky paths and steep climbs. When you reach the tea house, you'll be greeted with a breathtaking view of the lake below, and you can enjoy a warm cup of tea before heading back down. This ride is best suited for those with some riding experience, as the terrain can be tricky at times, but it's one of the most scenic rides in the area.

Horseback riding in Banff is a chance to see the national park in a completely different way. The slower pace allows you to fully appreciate the beauty of the Rockies, and riding a horse through the wilderness feels like you're stepping into a different time. Just be sure to wear comfortable clothing, bring a water bottle, and don't forget your camera – the views you'll see along the way are worth capturing. Riding through Banff's trails, with nothing but the sounds of your horse's hooves and the wind in the trees, is an experience that truly allows you to connect with the heart of this magnificent landscape.

Helicopter Tours Over the Rockies

Helicopter tours over the Canadian Rockies offer a thrilling and unforgettable way to experience the breathtaking scenery of Banff and its surrounding landscapes. There's something truly special about soaring high above the rugged peaks, turquoise lakes, and thick forests, giving you a bird's-eye view that can't be seen from the ground. Whether you're a first-time visitor or a regular in the area, a helicopter tour adds a new dimension to your adventure, letting you take in the vastness of the mountains and the pristine beauty of the wilderness below.

One of the top companies offering helicopter tours in the Rockies is Alpine Helicopters, located at 91 Bow Valley Trail, Canmore, AB T1W 1N8. Just a 20-minute drive from Banff, this company provides several tour options depending on how long you want to be in the air. It's very easy to get to the heliport in Canmore, and the staff is friendly, ensuring that you feel safe and excited for the flight. When I first arrived, I was struck by how professional everything felt, from the safety briefing to the equipment. They truly make sure you're comfortable before taking off.

If you're short on time, the Three Sisters Peaks Tour is a fantastic choice. This 12-minute flight takes you above the iconic Three Sisters mountain range, a famous trio of peaks in the Bow Valley. As soon as we lifted off, the sense of awe was immediate. The helicopter glided smoothly through the air, and the views were incredible — I couldn't believe how small everything looked below. The pilot provided fascinating commentary on the area's history and geology, making the experience both thrilling and informative.

For a more extended experience, I recommend the Royal Canadian Tour, which lasts about 30 minutes. This tour takes you deeper into the mountains, flying over remote valleys, high alpine lakes, and glaciers that are hidden from the roads and trails. One of the highlights for me was flying over the Spray Lakes Reservoir, a huge body of shimmering blue water nestled between the mountains. The views were simply stunning, and seeing the glaciers from above gave me a true appreciation of the raw beauty of the Rockies. The helicopter allows you to get close to some of the most spectacular ice fields in the region, and even though you're moving fast, it never feels rushed — there's plenty of time to take in the scenery.

For those who want to go all out, the Mt. Assiniboine Glacier Tour is an absolute must. This 42-minute flight takes you all the way to the Matterhorn of the Rockies — Mt. Assiniboine. This towering peak sits at over 3,600 meters and is often surrounded by clouds, making it a striking sight from the air. During the tour, you'll also get views of Lake Louise, Moraine Lake, and the Victoria Glacier, some of the most famous natural landmarks in Banff National Park. I was speechless for most of the flight — there's something surreal about hovering over these massive landscapes and realizing how immense and untouched they are.

Another popular option is with Rockies Heli Canada, which operates near Abraham Lake, about an hour and a half from Banff at Cline River Heliport, David Thompson Hwy, Nordegg,

AB ToM 2H0. They offer a mix of scenic tours and adventure packages. One of their unique options is combining a helicopter tour with hiking or snowshoeing in a remote alpine area. The Ultimate Heli-Hiking Adventure is a half-day experience where you're dropped off in a stunning backcountry location to explore on foot before being picked up later. I haven't tried this one yet, but it's high on my list because it combines the excitement of flight with the peace of a hike through untouched wilderness.

No matter which tour you choose, the experience is bound to be incredible. Banff's helicopter tours provide a unique perspective on the Rockies, offering views that few people ever get to see. It's perfect for photographers looking to capture epic shots, or for anyone who just wants to feel the thrill of soaring through the mountains. The helicopters are designed to give you great visibility, with large windows and comfortable seating, and the pilots are knowledgeable, often pointing out landmarks and wildlife as you fly.

If you plan to do a helicopter tour, remember to dress warmly, even in the summer months, as it can get chilly up in the mountains. I also recommend bringing a camera with a good zoom lens because you'll want to capture every moment of this once-in-a-lifetime experience.

Whether it's your first time in Banff or you've been visiting for years, seeing the Rockies from the air is a perspective you don't want to miss. It's a chance to truly understand the scale and majesty of this beautiful part of the world. The memories from that flight will stay with you long after you land.

CHAPTER ELEVEN

BANFF'S HIDDEN GEMS

Secret Trails and Off-the-Beaten-Path Lakes

Exploring secret trails and off-the-beaten-path lakes around Banff can make you feel like you've stumbled upon hidden treasures that most visitors never get to experience. These spots are quieter, more peaceful, and offer a sense of solitude that's often hard to find in such a popular destination. If you're looking to escape the crowds and dive into some of the lesser-known corners of the Canadian Rockies, these hidden gems are perfect for a more intimate adventure.

One of my favorite secret trails is the Baker Creek to Sawback Lake Trail. Located along the Bow Valley Parkway, Baker Creek is about a 20-minute drive west of Banff. You can start this hike near the Baker Creek Mountain Resort at Bow Valley Pkwy, Improvement District No. 9, AB T0L 1C0. The trail itself is not very well-marked, but that's what makes it feel like a true hidden escape. As you walk through dense forest and cross bubbling streams, you'll hardly see anyone else. The hike can be moderately challenging at times, but the reward comes when you arrive at Sawback Lake, a pristine, quiet lake surrounded by towering peaks. Sitting by the water, listening to the sounds of nature with no one else around, makes you feel like you've discovered a secret sanctuary.

Another wonderful hidden lake is Boom Lake, nestled near the Alberta-British Columbia border. To get here, drive about 40 minutes west of Banff along the Trans-Canada Highway, then take the exit for Boom Lake Trailhead at Highway 93,

Improvement District No. 9, AB ToL 1E0. The trail is around 5 kilometers one way, winding through the forest before opening up to reveal the serene, turquoise waters of Boom Lake. The best part is how uncrowded it usually is, even on weekends. When I first visited Boom Lake, I was struck by the stillness of the water, reflecting the surrounding cliffs like a mirror. It's an ideal spot to bring a picnic, relax by the shoreline, and even dip your toes in the cool glacial water on a warm day.

For something truly off the beaten path, head to Taylor Lake. This trail is located about 15 minutes west of Lake Louise, with the trailhead at Taylor Lake Parking Lot, Highway 1, Improvement District No. 9, AB ToL 1E0. The hike to Taylor Lake is roughly 6 kilometers each way and is moderately difficult, taking you through thick woods and offering glimpses of the surrounding mountains as you climb. When I reached Taylor Lake, I was surprised by how quiet it was — it felt like a hidden alpine paradise. The water is a beautiful emerald green, and the surrounding meadows are filled with wildflowers in the summer. It's a fantastic place to enjoy a picnic or just sit and soak in the views. If you're lucky, you might even spot some wildlife, like deer or mountain goats, along the way.

For those wanting an even more adventurous experience, Paradise Valley is an excellent option. Though it's less famous than nearby Lake Louise or Moraine Lake, Paradise Valley offers an incredible hiking experience without the crowds. To access it, you'll start at the Moraine Lake Road parking lot, about 14 kilometers from Lake Louise Village. The trail leads you deep into the valley, where towering peaks and glacial streams surround you. My favorite part of this hike is the hidden Giant Steps Waterfall, a series of cascading falls that feels like something out of a fairy tale. Most visitors to the area never make it this far, so it's a peaceful and breathtaking reward for those willing to explore a little farther.

If you're seeking complete solitude, head to Bourgeau Lake. The trailhead is located at Sunshine Village Access Road, Trans-Canada Highway, Banff, AB ToL oCo, about 15 minutes from Banff. This 7.5-kilometer hike is fairly challenging but incredibly rewarding. The trail winds through dense forest before reaching the stunning alpine Bourgeau Lake, surrounded by rugged mountain peaks. I love coming here for the solitude and the chance to see alpine wildlife. If you have extra energy, you can continue on to Harvey Pass for even more breathtaking views of the surrounding valleys.

When exploring these hidden gems, it's essential to be well-prepared, as these trails are often less maintained and marked than the popular routes. Make sure to carry a detailed map, plenty of water, snacks, and bear spray, as wildlife is more commonly seen in these quieter areas. And, as always, remember to leave no trace, taking all your trash with you and respecting the pristine environment.

Finding these secret trails and lakes feels like uncovering a side of Banff that many visitors miss. Each of these spots offers a unique opportunity to connect with nature, away from the crowds, and enjoy the peaceful beauty of the Canadian Rockies. Whether you're looking for a quiet picnic spot or a challenging hike, these off-the-beaten-path locations provide a sense of adventure and discovery that's hard to beat.

Local's Favorite Spots for Tranquility

When you want to escape the crowds and find a peaceful corner of Banff, it's the locals who know the best spots for tranquility. These hidden gems are often overlooked by tourists but provide some of the most serene and relaxing experiences in the area. Whether you're looking for a quiet place to reflect, enjoy nature, or simply relax, these local favorites offer just that.

One of the most beloved spots for peace and quiet is Vermilion Lakes, located just outside the town of Banff. You can reach them by driving along Vermilion Lakes Road, which is about a five-minute drive from downtown Banff. The road winds along three tranquil lakes, with breathtaking views of Mount Rundle in the background. This area is perfect for a peaceful walk, a quiet paddle, or simply sitting by the water to watch the sunset. I love coming here in the early morning when the water is still, and you can see the reflection of the mountains on the surface. It's a great spot to soak in the beauty of Banff without the hustle and bustle of the more touristy areas.

Another local favorite for tranquility is Johnson Lake, located about 15 minutes from Banff along the Lake Minnewanka Scenic Drive. This small, calm lake is surrounded by forest and has a gentle trail that loops around the water. It's a perfect place for a quiet afternoon walk or a relaxing picnic. On warm summer days, you might even see locals swimming in the clear, cool water. Unlike the busy beaches of Lake Minnewanka, Johnson Lake remains much quieter, making it a peaceful escape. I've often come here with a book and spent hours sitting by the shoreline, listening to the birds and the soft rustle of the trees.

If you're looking for a place to connect with nature while staying away from the crowds, head to Cascade Ponds. Located just off the Trans-Canada Highway, it's a quick 10-minute drive from Banff. The ponds are surrounded by picnic tables, fire pits, and scenic views of Cascade Mountain. This spot is popular with locals who want a peaceful afternoon by the water, whether for a barbecue, a short walk, or just to relax with friends and family. I've spent many quiet afternoons here, enjoying the stillness of the water and the surrounding wilderness.

For those who want to explore a bit farther from town, Fenland Loop is a great choice. This short and easy trail is located just outside Banff, near the Banff Recreation Grounds. The trail winds through a peaceful forest and along a quiet stream, making it the perfect spot for a leisurely walk. It's a local favorite because of its tranquility and easy accessibility. Even on weekends, you can find moments of complete solitude along this trail, surrounded by the sounds of nature. I often take a stroll here when I need a break from the busier areas of Banff and want to reconnect with the peacefulness of the forest.

If you're looking for a truly serene experience, Lake Agnes above Lake Louise is a hidden gem. While Lake Louise itself can be crowded, the hike up to Lake Agnes is often much quieter, especially in the early morning or late afternoon. The hike is moderate, about 3.5 kilometers one way, and takes you to a beautiful alpine lake with a charming tea house. Once you reach Lake Agnes, you'll be rewarded with stunning views of the lake and surrounding mountains, all while enjoying the peaceful atmosphere. I recommend arriving early to have the place to yourself — it's a magical experience to sip tea by the lake with nothing but the sound of the wind and water around you.

Each of these spots offers a chance to unwind, relax, and experience the natural beauty of Banff without the crowds. Whether you're looking for a quiet walk, a peaceful place to sit, or a spot to enjoy a picnic, these local favorites provide the perfect escape for anyone seeking tranquility in the heart of the Canadian Rockies.

Unique Experiences (Ghost Walks, Stargazing)

If you're looking for something a little different while exploring Banff, there are some truly unique experiences that will add an exciting and memorable twist to your visit. Two of the most intriguing are ghost walks and stargazing, which offer both a connection to the region's mysterious past and the stunning beauty of its nighttime skies.

One of the most fascinating ways to dive into Banff's history is through a ghost walk. These guided tours are a fun way to explore the town's eerie past, uncovering tales of haunted hotels, spooky encounters, and strange events. The Banff Ghost Walk is popular among locals and visitors alike, offering a spooky yet entertaining way to see the town after dark. The tour typically begins at 137 Banff Avenue, right in the heart of town, and takes you through various historic sites. Along the way, you'll hear chilling stories of Banff's ghostly residents, including long-forgotten figures who still linger in some of the town's oldest buildings. Whether you believe in ghosts or not, it's a fun way to learn about the region's past, all while seeing the town from a different perspective. As you wander the quiet streets, lit by dim lamps, the mountains looming in the background, you'll feel a sense of the eerie and mysterious that only comes out at night.

I've been on the ghost walk a couple of times, and what really makes it special is how the stories bring Banff's history to life. Hearing about the haunted rooms of the Banff Springs Hotel or the strange sightings along the Bow River Trail gives the town a completely new and exciting atmosphere. It's a great experience for anyone who enjoys a bit of mystery and loves hearing local legends.

For a completely different kind of adventure, stargazing in Banff is something you absolutely have to try. With the park's low light pollution and high elevation, Banff offers some of the clearest night skies you'll ever see. On a clear night, the sky becomes a canvas full of stars, and you can often spot constellations, planets, and even the Milky Way stretching across the sky. One of the best spots for stargazing is Two Jack Lake, about a 15-minute drive from Banff along the Lake Minnewanka Loop. Here, the open skies and reflection of the stars on the lake's surface create a breathtaking scene. You can drive right up to the lake, park your car, and set up a cozy spot by the water to watch the night sky unfold.

Another great location is Lake Minnewanka itself, a bit farther down the road from Two Jack Lake. This area is known for its wide, unobstructed views of the sky and its peaceful surroundings, making it a perfect place to lay back and enjoy the stars. On clear nights, you might even catch a glimpse of the northern lights dancing across the horizon. I've spent many nights stargazing here, bundled up in a blanket with a thermos of hot chocolate, just enjoying the silence and the beauty above. It's an unforgettable experience that really makes you feel connected to the natural world.

If you're keen on learning more about the night sky, Banff National Park also offers guided stargazing experiences, especially during the fall months. These tours often include telescopes, professional astronomers, and fascinating facts about the stars and planets. I once joined a guided stargazing session, and it was amazing to see the rings of Saturn and the craters on the moon through a telescope. The guide's knowledge made it even more special, pointing out constellations and sharing stories of how different cultures have viewed the stars over the centuries.

Both ghost walks and stargazing in Banff offer unique ways to experience the park beyond the usual hiking and sightseeing. Whether you're exploring the haunted corners of town or gazing up at the endless stars in the clear mountain sky, these activities will leave you with unforgettable memories. They're perfect for anyone who loves a good story, enjoys a bit of mystery, or simply wants to marvel at the beauty of the world around them.

CHAPTER TWELVE
PRACTICAL INFORMATION

Money matters and Currency Exchange

The currency used in Banff National Park, located in Canada, is the Canadian Dollar (CAD), not the Euro. Understanding the local currency and budgeting for your trip is essential to make the most of your visit to Banff's stunning landscapes. Let's take a look at the currency exchange options, budgeting tips, payment methods, and some personal insights to help you navigate the financial side of your trip with ease.

When it comes to exchanging currency, there are a few key options available to travelers in Banff. One of the best ways to get Canadian dollars is through ATMs, which are widely available throughout Banff. These machines often offer favorable exchange rates, although it's important to check with your bank regarding any foreign transaction fees that might be applied. Some of the main banks in the area, like RBC (Royal Bank of Canada) and TD Canada Trust, have ATMs that accept international cards. Another option is using currency exchange offices, but these may charge higher fees or offer less competitive rates. You'll find currency exchange services in Calgary, which is the nearest large city, as well as in Banff itself. While it's convenient to exchange money at airports, the rates are often less favorable, so it's better to avoid this option unless absolutely necessary.

Budgeting for your trip to Banff can vary greatly depending on your preferences and the experiences you're looking for. For travelers on a budget, accommodation at hostels or basic motels can range from CAD 60 to 120 per night. Meals at more affordable spots or casual dining places may cost around CAD 15 to 25 per person. If you're mid-range, you'll find hotels in the CAD 150 to 250 per night range, while dining in sit-down restaurants might cost about CAD 30 to 50 per meal. For a more luxurious experience, expect to pay upwards of CAD 300 per night at high-end hotels, with meals at fine dining establishments costing around CAD 60 or more per person. Activities like hiking are free or low-cost, but guided tours, wildlife viewing trips, or special experiences like helicopter tours can range from CAD 100 to 400, depending on the service.

Payment methods in Banff are straightforward. Credit and debit cards are widely accepted, particularly Visa and MasterCard, which are commonly used across Canada. American Express is accepted at many places, but it's less universal than the other two. If you're visiting smaller cafes, local shops, or outdoor markets, it's a good idea to carry some cash, as not all places accept cards. ATMs are available throughout the town for cash withdrawals, though it's worth keeping in mind that foreign transaction fees may apply. There aren't any specific local payment apps you need to worry about, as card payments are dominant and widely accepted.

When you're budgeting for Banff, it's helpful to know a little about local pricing trends. During the peak summer months, particularly July and August, accommodation and activity prices can surge due to the high influx of tourists. Similarly, winter, particularly around ski season in December and January, sees higher costs for both lodging and activities. If you're looking to save money, consider visiting during the shoulder seasons, like early fall or late spring, when the crowds are fewer, and prices tend to drop. Additionally, dining in local favorite spots, rather than in the more touristy areas, can save you a bit of money. For example, eating at a local pub or diner might be much more affordable compared to the upscale restaurants along Banff Avenue, and the food is still delicious and hearty. It's also worth noting that some activities, such as park entrance fees, are fixed, but guided tours or equipment rentals may have hidden costs that can add up, so it's good to ask in advance.

I once found myself short on cash during a trip to Banff when I realized the small café I wanted to eat at didn't accept credit cards. Thankfully, I was able to find an ATM nearby, but the fees were higher than I expected. From that experience, I learned to always carry a small amount of local currency, especially when visiting smaller or more remote locations. Another lesson came from underestimating the price surge during peak season. I had planned to visit in July and was shocked by the jump in accommodation prices compared to the previous fall. Booking ahead during high season and being mindful of seasonal changes can save you from these surprises.

For managing your budget and keeping track of expenses, several tools and resources can be helpful. Budgeting apps like Trail Wallet or XE Currency can help you keep track of your spending in real time, while websites like Trivago or Booking.com are excellent for finding accommodation deals. Currency converters like OANDA or the XE app are also great to have on hand, ensuring you're aware of current exchange rates before making large transactions. I've found it useful to set a daily spending limit on my budgeting app, especially in Banff where you might be tempted to splurge on activities like helicopter tours or fine dining.

By planning ahead, understanding your currency exchange options, and budgeting for your preferred travel style, you can fully enjoy your time in Banff without stressing over money matters. From managing your cash flow to keeping an eye on seasonal price shifts, a little preparation can go a long way toward making your trip smooth and financially stress-free.

Language and Communication

In Banff National Park, the primary language spoken is English, which is the dominant language throughout Canada. However, due to the park's rich cultural diversity and its popularity among international visitors, you'll also encounter some Italian and German speakers, especially in tourist areas. While the presence of these languages isn't as pronounced as in other regions, knowing a few phrases can enhance your interactions and show respect for the different cultures that come together in this stunning national park.

Basic greetings and polite phrases are essential for any traveler looking to connect with locals. In Italian, "hello" is "ciao" (pronounced chow) and "thank you" is "grazie" (pronounced grah-tsee-eh). "Please" translates to "per favore" (pronounced per fah-voh-ray), and "excuse me" is "mi scusi" (pronounced mee skoo-zee). In German, you can greet someone with "hallo" (pronounced hah-loh), say "thank you" with "danke" (pronounced dahn-keh), use "bitte" (pronounced bih-teh) for "please," and for "excuse me," you can say "entschuldigung" (pronounced ent-shool-dee-goong). Familiarizing yourself with these simple phrases can make a big difference in your interactions.

As you navigate through Banff, having practical phrases at your disposal is beneficial. When ordering food, you might say, "Vorrei questo, per favore," in Italian, meaning "I would like this, please." In German, you could ask, "Ich hätte gerne das," which also means "I would like that." If you need to ask for directions, try "Dove si trova...?" in Italian, meaning "Where is...?" or "Wo ist...?" in German. For making purchases, knowing how to ask, "Quanto costa?" in Italian (meaning "How much does it cost?") or "Wie viel kostet das?" in German can be handy. If you find yourself in need of assistance, "Hai bisogno di aiuto?" in Italian (meaning "Do you need help?") or "Brauchen Sie Hilfe?" in German can facilitate communication.

For those interested in learning some of these essential phrases before or during their trip, several resources can be quite helpful. Mobile apps like Duolingo and Babbel offer beginner courses in Italian and German, making it easy to pick up essential vocabulary and phrases. Phrasebooks tailored to travelers can also be found at local bookstores or online retailers, providing you with a quick reference guide for common expressions. Websites like Memrise offer user-friendly lessons that cover practical language skills, perfect for getting ready for your Banff adventure.

Understanding cultural nuances is vital in any travel experience. In Banff, while English is the primary language, politeness and respect are universal. Using formal language when addressing someone for the first time is always appreciated, especially in service contexts. For instance, saying "Signore" (Mr.) or "Signora" (Mrs.) in Italian, or "Herr" and "Frau" in German can add a touch of respect in conversations. Additionally, maintaining good eye contact and a friendly demeanor can go a long way in establishing rapport. Gestures like a nod or a smile are understood universally and can help convey warmth and friendliness.

While English-speaking staff are readily available at major tourist attractions, hotels, and restaurants, it's reassuring to know that multilingual assistance exists in Banff. Many staff members are trained to communicate with international visitors, making it easier to find help. If you're looking for someone who speaks Italian or German, simply ask at the front desk of your hotel or the visitor information center, and they will do their best to accommodate you.

Respecting the local languages and cultures is essential. By making an effort to learn and use basic phrases, you demonstrate appreciation for the diverse community that exists in Banff National Park. Whether it's exchanging greetings with a local or trying out a few phrases with fellow travelers, these small gestures enrich your experience and help foster connections.

With a little preparation, you can enhance your visit to Banff National Park. Embracing the local languages, even if just a few phrases, opens doors to deeper interactions and a more memorable journey in this beautiful part of the world.

Safety and Health

Planning a trip to Banff National Park is exciting, but it's important to keep safety and health in mind to ensure a smooth and enjoyable experience. This stunning region, known for its breathtaking landscapes and outdoor adventures, also requires travelers to be mindful of their surroundings and take necessary precautions.

General safety tips for visitors start with being aware of your surroundings. It's easy to get lost in the beauty of the park, but maintaining awareness can help you avoid risky areas, especially near wildlife or steep cliffs. Always stay on marked trails and respect local customs, including wildlife guidelines, which emphasize not approaching or feeding animals. Familiarizing yourself with park regulations can also enhance your experience and ensure you're following the rules that protect both visitors and the environment.

When enjoying outdoor activities like hiking, skiing, or climbing, specific safety considerations come into play. Before heading out, always check the weather conditions. The weather in the mountains can change quickly, so look for updates on local forecasts or park advisories. Understanding trail markers is crucial; they provide information on difficulty levels and direction. If you experience symptoms of altitude sickness, such as headaches, dizziness, or nausea, it's vital to take these seriously and descend to a lower elevation.

Health precautions are key in ensuring a safe trip. Staying hydrated is essential, especially during physical activities. Carry enough water and drink regularly, as dehydration can sneak up on you in the dry mountain air. Using sunscreen is crucial too, as UV rays are stronger at higher altitudes. Layering your clothing is a smart strategy since temperatures can vary throughout the day. Make sure to wear moisture-wicking fabrics that can help regulate your body temperature. While there aren't specific vaccinations required for visiting Banff, it's always a good idea to be up-to-date on routine vaccinations.

In case of an emergency, knowing how to access local services is vital. The emergency number in Canada is 911, which connects you to local emergency services, including police, fire, and medical assistance. The nearest hospital to Banff is the Banff Mineral Springs Hospital, located at 305 Lynx St, Banff, AB T1L 1H7. For outdoor rescue services, Parks Canada has a dedicated emergency response team that can assist in mountain rescues. If you need their help, you can reach them via the Banff Visitor Centre at 403-762-1550.

Travel insurance is an essential aspect of any trip, particularly for outdoor adventures in places like Banff. Look for a policy that covers health and safety issues, including emergency medical expenses and evacuation services. It's a good idea to read the fine print to understand what is covered, especially for activities like skiing or climbing, which may require additional coverage.

Local health services are available in Banff, including pharmacies and clinics. For minor health issues, the Banff Health Centre at 123 Bear St is a convenient option. There are also pharmacies like the Shoppers Drug Mart at 1110 Bow

Valley Trail, where you can find basic medications and supplies. It's helpful to know that if you need medical care, you should always bring your health insurance card and any necessary identification.

To help you stay informed and safe during your visit, consider downloading safety apps like MyAltitudes, which can track your elevation and help monitor for altitude sickness. Websites like the Banff National Park site provide updates on trail conditions, wildlife warnings, and emergency contacts. Having a physical map of the park can also be beneficial, especially in areas where cell service may be limited.

By prioritizing safety and health during your trip to Banff National Park, you can fully immerse yourself in the stunning surroundings while minimizing risks. Taking the time to prepare will allow you to focus on enjoying your adventure in this breathtaking corner of Canada.

Emergency Contacts

When visiting the breathtaking Banff National Park, being prepared for emergencies is essential. The park has a robust system of emergency services designed to respond to various situations, ensuring the safety of both visitors and residents. Emergency services, including police, fire, and medical, operate efficiently in both urban areas like Banff town and the more remote regions of the park. The staff is trained to handle everything from minor incidents to serious emergencies, and they work closely with Parks Canada to ensure the safety of all.

It's crucial to be familiar with essential emergency phone numbers. The general emergency number for Banff National Park is 911. This connects you to all emergency services, whether you need police, fire, or medical assistance. The local police can be reached at the Banff Detachment, where they can assist with any safety concerns or issues. For ambulance services, calling 911 will dispatch paramedics to your location. The fire department is also contacted through 911 for any fire-related emergencies. If you're in a remote area and require mountain rescue services, it's best to let 911 know so they can send specialized teams equipped for wilderness rescues.

If you find yourself in need of medical assistance, several hospitals and clinics are available in and around Banff National Park. The Banff Mineral Springs Hospital, located at 305 Lynx St, Banff, AB T1L 1H7, offers emergency medical services and general health care. You can reach them at 403-762-2222. For minor ailments or prescriptions, the Shoppers Drug Mart pharmacy at 1110 Bow Valley Trail is a convenient stop. In Canmore, which is just outside the park, the Canmore General Hospital provides additional medical services, located at 1100 Hospital Place, Canmore, AB T1W 1N5, with a contact number of 403-678-5500.

In the event of an emergency, knowing how to communicate your needs is crucial. When calling for help, provide clear and concise information, including your location, the nature of the emergency, and any specific details that might assist responders. If you're in a remote area, mention landmarks or trail markers that can help them find you more quickly. Language barriers may arise, but remaining calm and polite can help facilitate communication. Using simple phrases or gestures can often bridge the gap.

Travel insurance is another vital aspect of your trip to Banff. It's important to choose a policy that covers medical emergencies, including hospital stays and evacuation services. Before you travel, take time to research your insurance provider's emergency assistance services. Many companies offer 24/7 helplines, which can help guide you through the process of accessing care when needed.

Personal safety tips for outdoor activities are essential to ensure a fun experience. Always carry a first aid kit with basic supplies, and consider including items like blister pads, antiseptic wipes, and any personal medications. It's a good idea to inform someone about your plans, including your intended route and expected return time. This way, if something goes wrong, someone will know to alert authorities if you don't return as expected.

In Banff, cultural nuances can play a role in seeking help. Canadians are generally polite and approachable, so don't hesitate to ask locals for assistance if you need it. It's important to be courteous and respectful, as this fosters a positive interaction.

Consider a scenario where a traveler, excited to explore a remote hiking trail, slips and twists an ankle. They had informed their friend about their plans and the estimated time for their return. Realizing they couldn't walk back, they used their mobile phone to call 911, providing their exact location using a nearby trail marker. The emergency responders were able to reach them quickly due to the clear information provided. This experience taught them the importance of preparation and communication in outdoor adventures.

To help you stay prepared, consider downloading emergency apps that provide information on local services, trail conditions, and emergency contacts. Websites like the Parks Canada site offer updates on park safety, wildlife warnings, and other essential information for your visit.

By being informed about emergency contacts and procedures, you can enhance your experience in Banff National Park while prioritizing safety. Preparation and awareness can make all the difference, allowing you to focus on enjoying the stunning beauty of this remarkable destination.

Useful Websites and Apps

Planning a trip to Banff National Park is an adventure in itself, and having the right apps can enhance your experience and help you navigate this stunning region with ease. From transportation to outdoor activities, the right tools can make your journey smoother and more enjoyable.

When it comes to essential apps, a few stand out for anyone looking to explore Banff. Transportation apps like Google Maps or Waze are invaluable for navigating the area, especially if you're driving. They provide real-time traffic updates, route options, and even information about parking availability. For accommodation, apps like Booking.com and Airbnb allow you to compare prices, read reviews, and find the perfect place to stay, whether you're looking for a cozy cabin or a hotel with a view. Dining apps like TripAdvisor can guide you to the best local eateries based on user reviews, ensuring you don't miss out on Banff's culinary delights.

For those eager to hit the trails, hiking and outdoor apps are essential. AllTrails offers an extensive database of trail maps, detailed descriptions, and user reviews, helping you choose hikes that match your skill level. With AllTrails, you can download maps for offline use, which is a lifesaver when exploring remote areas with limited signal. Gaia GPS is another fantastic option, providing comprehensive topographic maps and navigation tools to ensure you stay on track. ViewRanger enhances your hiking experience with features like augmented reality, which can help you identify mountain peaks and other landmarks along your route. These apps also offer weather forecasts, ensuring you're prepared for changing conditions.

Staying connected with locals and navigating the park can sometimes pose a challenge, especially if language differences arise. Language and translation apps like Google Translate can help you understand menus, signs, and conversations, making it easier to engage with the community. Duolingo is great for learning basic phrases in English or other languages, enhancing your interactions with locals. iTranslate also offers voice translation, which can be particularly useful in conversations.

Safety is paramount, and several apps can help you stay informed and prepared for emergencies. The First Aid app by the American Red Cross is a fantastic resource, offering step-by-step instructions for common first aid situations. It also provides emergency contact information and safety tips tailored to outdoor activities. GeoSure Travel Safety gives you insights into various safety factors, such as crime rates and health risks, helping you make informed decisions about where to explore.

To immerse yourself in the rich cultural and historical context of the park, consider downloading apps that provide insights into its heritage. Apps like Dolomiti UNESCO and Dolomiti Superski offer guided tours and information about the area's natural wonders and cultural significance. These apps can enhance your understanding of the stunning landscapes you'll encounter.

One key aspect to remember when exploring Banff National Park is the possibility of limited internet access in remote areas. This is where offline capabilities become essential. Before you travel, download maps, guides, and any other important information to ensure you have access even without a connection. Most outdoor apps, like AllTrails and Gaia GPS, allow you to save maps for offline use, making them incredibly useful.

To make the most of your apps while traveling, ensure your devices are fully charged before heading out, and consider carrying a portable charger for long days of exploration. Be mindful of data usage, especially if you're traveling internationally, as roaming charges can quickly add up. Downloading content while connected to Wi-Fi can help you save on data costs.

Equipping yourself with the right apps can significantly enhance your experience in Banff National Park. Whether you're navigating the roads, exploring hiking trails, or learning about the local culture, these tools will help you make the most of your adventure in this breathtaking wilderness. Embrace the journey and let these apps guide you through the stunning landscapes and rich experiences that await in Banff.

CONCLUSION

As you prepare to embark on your journey through Banff National Park, it's essential to reflect on the unique experiences that await you in this breathtaking destination. Banff is not just a feast for the eyes; it's a harmonious blend of natural beauty, thrilling outdoor adventures, rich cultural experiences, and culinary delights that leave a lasting impression. Imagine standing before the turquoise waters of Lake Louise, surrounded by towering peaks that seem to touch the sky, or hiking through the pristine wilderness where every turn reveals a new wonder. This is a place where the mountains whisper tales of ancient glaciers, and the air is filled with the scent of pine and adventure.

My own journey in Banff has been nothing short of transformative. I recall the first time I stood atop a summit after a challenging hike. The view was awe-inspiring, but it was the sense of achievement and connection to nature that truly moved me. It's moments like these that inspire a sense of wonder and appreciation for the world around us. Banff invites you to explore its vastness, to immerse yourself in its serene landscapes, and to feel the pulse of life that thrives within its borders. Each experience here has the potential to ignite your spirit of adventure and remind you of the beauty of the natural world.

I encourage you to step outside your comfort zone while in Banff. Perhaps you'll tackle a challenging trail that rewards you with panoramic views or dive into the local cuisine, sampling dishes that reflect the region's cultural heritage. Engaging with the local community, whether through art, music, or traditional events, can deepen your connection to the land and its people. The rewards of these experiences often outweigh the initial hesitation, leaving you with unforgettable memories and stories to share.

While the iconic sights of Banff, such as Moraine Lake and the Banff Gondola, are undeniably breathtaking, don't overlook the hidden gems that await you beyond the well-trodden paths. Take the time to explore lesser-known trails, visit quaint local shops, and engage in community events. These experiences often lead to the most memorable moments of your trip, providing a deeper understanding of the region's culture and environment.

As you navigate through this stunning park, consider the importance of sustainable travel practices. Respecting the environment by adhering to park guidelines, minimizing waste, and supporting local businesses is crucial in preserving the beauty of Banff for generations to come. By engaging in responsible tourism, you contribute to the conservation of this precious landscape while enriching your own experience.

To enhance your journey, plan ahead but also remain open to spontaneity. Engage with locals for recommendations on hidden spots, and don't hesitate to veer off your planned route when something catches your eye. Each moment spent in Banff is an opportunity for exploration and discovery.

I invite you to share your experiences and stories from Banff, whether through social media or travel blogs. The value of community and shared experiences enriches our understanding of this beautiful region. Your stories can inspire others to embark on their own adventures and discover the magic of Banff National Park.

In closing, let the beauty of adventure inspire you as you explore Banff National Park. The memories you create here will last a lifetime, shaping your appreciation for nature and the wonders it holds. As you journey through this breathtaking region, remember that every trail hiked, every meal savored, and every connection made adds to the tapestry of your experience. Embrace the journey ahead, and may your time in Banff be filled with awe, joy, and unforgettable moments.

MAP/BONUS

Scan QR Code with device to view map for easy navigation

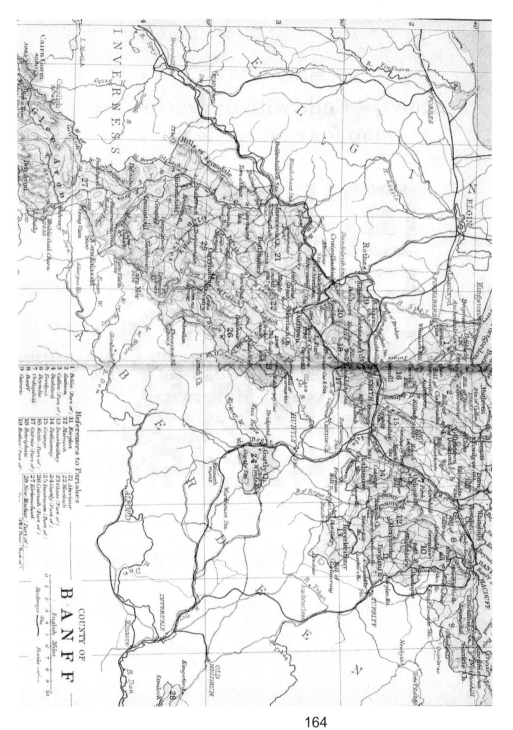

COUNTY OF
B A N F F

References to Parishes

1 Boltie (Part of)
2 Aucton
3 Cullen (Part of)
4 Deskford
5 Fordyce
6 Keith (Part of)
7 Ordiquhill
8 Banff
9 Gamrie
11 Forglen
12 Marnoch
13 Inverkeithny
14 Rothiemay
15 Grange
16 Keith (Part of)
17 Cairnie (Part of)
18 Botriphnie
19 Rathvie (Part of)
22 Aberlour
23 Mortlach
23 Glass (Part of)
24 Gartly (Part of)
25 Inveraven (Part of)
26 Kirkmichael (Part of)
27 Kirkmichael (Part of)
28 New Machar (Part of)
29 Rayne (Part of)

English Miles
0 1 2 3 4 5 6 7 8 9 10

Railways Stns

Roads

Daily *Journal*

Daily  Journal

Daily Journal

Daily Journal

Daily  Journal

Banff National Park through my eyes

Banff National Park through my eyes

Made in the USA
Middletown, DE
24 February 2025

71827304R00095